GREETING THE ANGELS:

An Imaginal View of the Mourning Process

GREETING THE ANGELS:

An Imaginal View of the Mourning Process

Greg Mogenson

Death, Value and Meaning Series
Series Editor: John D. Morgan

Baywood Publishing Company, Inc.
AMITYVILLE, NEW YORK

Library of Congress Catalog Number: 91-35847
ISBN: 0-89503-096-9 (Paper)
ISBN: 0-89503-097-7 (Cloth)

Library of Congress Cataloging-in-Publication Data

Mogenson, Greg, 1959-
Greeting the angels : an imaginal view of the mourning process / Greg Mogenson.
p. cm. -- (Death, value, and meaning series)
Includes bibliographical references and index.
ISBN 0-89503-097-7. -- ISBN 0-89503-096-9 (pbk.)
1. Bereavement--Psychological aspects. 2. Death--Psychological aspects. 3. Loss (Psychology) 4. Grief. 5. Imagery (Psychology) I. Title. II. Series.
BF575.G7M64 1992
155.9'37--dc20 91-35847
CIP

Gods whose dominion is over the Souls, Shades without sound, Void, and you Burning River, and you broad Spaces voiceless beneath the Night, may I remain sinless in telling what has been told me, and, by your divine assent, reveal truth sunk in depths of earth and gloom.

Virgil, *The Aeneid*, Bk VI

O me, why have they not buried me deep enough?
Is it kind to have made me a grave so rough,
Me, that was never a quiet sleeper?
Maybe still I am but half-dead;
Then I cannot be wholly dumb.
I will cry to the steps above my head
And somebody, surely, some kind heart will come
To bury me, bury me
Deeper, ever so little deeper.

Alfred Lord Tennyson, "Maud," XI

. . . he who remains passive when overwhelmed with grief loses his best chance of recovering elasticity of mind.

Charles Darwin,
The Expression of the Emotions in Man and Animals

Acknowledgments

While working on this book and, indeed, on earlier works, I have benefitted from almost daily conversation with my friend and mentor, Ross Woodman. His responses to my formulations, his knack for placing ideas in a larger context, and his allegiance to the dark side of the soul has inspired me again and again to extend my ideas and to develop new formulations. For his support and encouragement I am grateful.

My wife, Rita, has been another person of this work. By caring for me more unconditionally than for my words, she helped to clarify many confusions, allowing my mind to become a truer instrument of the heart. She was also a great help to me when preparing parts of the book for oral presentation.

Michael Mendis read the book in manuscript and helped me to express numerous ideas more clearly. He was also a great support while I was writing the last two chapters, especially in connection with the Christian ideas contained there.

Lastly, my father, Gordon Mogenson, whose illness coincided with the writing of this book, must also be appreciated. Much of what I understand about the "Kingdom of Ends" I have learned from him during this time.

An earlier version of "The Psychotherapy of the Dead: Loss and Character Structure in Freud's Metapsychology," was first published in *American Imago: A Psychoanalytic Journal of Culture, Science and the Arts,* 45:3, pp. 251-269, 1988.

A short version of "The Resurrection of the Dead: A Jungian Approach to the Mourning Process" was presented at the 1989 Death and Bereavement Conference, King's College, London, Ontario. In still another version it appeared in *The Journal of Analytical Psychology,* 35:3, pp. 317-334, 1990.

An earlier version of "Irreplaceable Objects: An Imaginal Approach to the Mourning of Inconsolable Losses" was presented at the 1989 Death and Bereavement Conference, King's College, London, Ontario and published among the conference proceedings.

A short version of "Bereavement Guilt" was presented at the 1991 Conference on Death Education, King's College, London, Ontario.

Greg Mogenson
London, Ontario

Table of Contents

Introduction

This book, written within the genre of imaginal psychology,[1] presents the *imaginal dimension* of the mourning process. As the title indicates, it addresses itself to the *images* which animate bereavement, the images of the dead. Like the ancient guidebooks of Tibet and Egypt, the emphasis in the pages which follow will be upon the souls of the dead and the manner in which their existence is continued in the mind. Though medical psychology defines mourning as the process by means of which the living detach themselves from the dead, the fantasies to which the bereaved are subject and the mythologies of the afterlife distributed throughout the world belie this definition. From the imaginal point of view, the end of life is not the end of soul. The images continue. Deep inside the grief of the bereaved, the dead are at work, making themselves into religion and culture, imagining themselves into soul.

Though the graveside would seem to be the place where we let go of the dead, it is also the place where we greet them again as angels. By returning to us in our dreams and fantasies, the dead assert their lasting value. Despite the fact that they are "gone," they continue to be the assumptions which underpin our lives. We cannot continue to know our own minds without continuing to have access to their images. The psyche is created, in large measure, by the mourning process itself. The more precisely we imagine our losses, the more psychological we

[1] The imaginal school of psychology is derived from the work of Jung on the one hand and from the work of Henry Corbin [1] on the other. Both thinkers place the imaginal psyche in the center of their concerns and recognize it as having ontological status in its own right. James Hillman is currently the leading contributor to this school. For a fuller account see a work by Roberts Avens [2].

become. We are the afterworld in which our loved ones dwell even as they are the cultural atmosphere in which we have our being. It is not simply that *they* live on in us; *we* live on in them as well.

The psychology of the mourning process resides in experiences and fantasies which begin beyond the grave. Mythologies of the afterworld, both personal and collective, present the epistemology of the psyche, the epistemology of the soul. Ideas such as 'heaven' and 'hell,' 'resurrection' and 'immortality' cannot be left out of the equation. They are the metaphors through which the psyche carries on. Though the life of the body is subject to decay, the imagination, unable to represent negation, perpetuates a *subtle body*. The blood which once flowed red through the veins of our loved ones now flows as ichor through the subtle arteries of the imaginal psyche.

Hiroshima, Nagasaki, Dachau, Auschwitz, Belfast, Tel Aviv, Jerusalem, Baghdad: cities of death, cities of soul. What Jung called the collective unconscious is an abyss of loss. Countless millions crowd the depths of the psyche waiting for the imagination to give them wings. "You could not find the ends of the soul, though you travelled its every way, so *deep* is its logos," writes Heraclitus [cited in 3, pp. 24-25]. The psyche is as deep and as logical as the graves from which it is resurrected. Little wonder it is so often insane. Will we ever awaken from the nightmare of history?

The way the dead appear to us in our dreams and fantasies, the things they say and do, present the logos of the psyche, the logic and culture of the mind, infinitely better than theories about the dynamic interaction of the institutions into which the mind has been mechanistically divided. The psychological complexity of the mourning process is missed if mourning is elucidated by a psychology other than the one which it is making with the dead. Mourning, we must never forget, is an intensely creative process. The bereaved must imagine their lost loved ones with the precision that makes for a successful elegy. Though bereavement has been divided into recognizable stages, no two instances of the mourning process are exactly alike. We mourn our losses differently, not merely because we are different, but because each loss is unique. The psychology of the mourning process is not exclusively a function of the bereaved; it is a function of the persons we are mourning as well. Our empathy, in this book, will be for them.

Though Freud was a principal proponent of the medical view of the mourning process, his own death bears witness to its imaginal dimension. As Auden expresses it in his elegy, "In Memory of Sigmund Freud,"

to us he is no more a person
now but a whole climate of opinion

under whom we conduct our different lives:
Like weather he can only hinder or help,
    the proud can still be proud but find it
a little harder, the tyrant tries to

make do with him but doesn't care for him much:
he quietly surrounds all our habits of growth
    and extends, till the tired in even
  the remotest miserable duchy

have felt the change in their bones and are cheered . . . [4, p. 217].

Whatever the merit of Freud's science of soul, we cannot understand ourselves today without recognizing its impact on us. Freud's theories are now an implicit part of our culture. Most of us in the present day recognize his ghost as real. Auden's observation is correct: "he is no more a person/ now but a whole climate of opinion."

Sigmund Freud, father of psychoanalysis, in a curious way you are our father too. Present in your absence, "quietly surround[ing] all our habits of growth," you continue to be a begetter of our souls. We are haunted by what you said and did. You continue to re-write yourself through the pens of your disciples. You have become the 'mental telepathy' which you wished you would have had another life to study.

Having appreciated Freud's contribution to our psychology, we must also delimit it. Others have died as well. Many, many others. I am not merely thinking of other analysts such as Jung, Adler or Melanie Klein—though they, too, have left permanent traces upon the psyche. Nor am I restricting my appreciation to epochal individuals such as Plato, Aristotle, Dante, Shakespeare, and Nietzsche, or to religious figures such as Abraham, Jesus, Mohammed, and Baha'u'llah—though it is true that much of our mental culture continues to be animated by their hearts and minds. I am thinking of dear ones closer to home. Fame is not a criterion for soul-making. Though the imaginal psyche has a poetic basis [5, pp. 6-10], it is not restricted to "the best and happiest moments of the happiest and best minds" [6, p. 1817]. Any loss can be a progenitor of the psyche. Parents and friends, siblings and children—anyone and everyone—becomes, through the act of dying, a father of psychoanalysis, a mother of soul. Every loss is worthy of an elegy. All creatures great and small are worthy of at least one stanza in "that great poem, which all poets," according to Shelley, "like the co-operating thoughts of one great mind, have built up since the beginning of the world" [cited in 7, p. 92].

Everything we mourn is generative of psyche, generative of soul. Whatever fails, dies, or is abandoned as error becomes an ancestor of consciousness. Yesterday's sciences, for example, are today's psychology.[2] As Jung has demonstrated, astrology and alchemy, though no longer of value as systems of contemporary science, present the psychology of the unconscious. Now that we no longer live with these systems as our truth we may acknowledge their value as psychic fictions or poetic truths. Like the fantasies into which a patient arranges the ink-blots on the Rorschach card, the exploded conventions of our earlier sciences reveal the fantasies which animate the soul. Maddening though it may be, the mind is full of images and concepts which our contemporary alchemies regard as mistaken, inferior, nonexistent, or dead. Psychology itself, the discipline, the "science," is a mourning process. Its theories, as Hillman has suggested, are also fantasy productions of the psyche [8, pp. 145-149]. Even when forcefully disputed, they continue to have a subtle validity. A theory of Jung's or Einstein's, a poem by Schiller, a prejudice of a crusty old uncle, the "oughts and shoulds" of mother, the witty ellipses of an inspiring professor—it's all psychology. The voices live on like Auden's and Freud's, regardless of the efforts of the living to dispute them.

The living and the dead inhabit a single community. It is not simply that we stand on the shoulders of giants. Like Aeneas carrying his father upon his back as he flees the fallen city of Troy, we bear the dead on our backs as well. History is not something we can simply bury and be done with. We are surrounded by it. The events and persons of the past become categories of the psyche, qualities of the NOW. What the Church calls the "Communion of Saints" is more than a creed. It is the imaginal dimension of everyday life. We bump into the shades of the past at every juncture. Failures of performance, slips of the tongue, lapses of penmanship, disturbances of attention—countless times each day we make unknowing sacrifices to the dead. Much of what we mistake for psychopathology is unconscious mourning. Though we wish to get on with the business of living, we cannot. Our last respects are simply not enough. The dead continue to demand attention. In unmarked graves called "symptoms," those whose value we have failed

[2] I am indebted to Prof. Ross Woodman for this observation.

to recognize rattle their chains. Until we let them into our present awareness, they cannot fully resurrect into their eternal lives.

It is not merely that the personal issues and conflicts *we* had with the dead linger on unresolved after death: The dead have unfinished business too, business which they pass along to us. Of course, it may be hard to recognize the current designs which the dead have upon us while we still have designs upon them. Indeed, it may be necessary to ruminate about old scores and assimilate projections for some time before we are ready to address the post mortem issues which the dead present. Eventually, however, we must free them from our feelings about the social roles they placed or failed to play in our lives and take up the larger questions in which their souls were/are tangled.

The meaning of our human existence stretches backwards into our ancestors and forwards into future generations. Indeed, the quality of the future we bequeath to our children depends, in large measure, upon the manner in which we have dealt with our ancestral ghosts. It is not enough to simply forget our late dear ones and walk psychopathically toward our own egoistic futures. We must continue to sense their influence upon our lives and to live in a manner that will have a redemptive influence on their souls as well. The meaning of life is something we find through the mourning of life lost. Indeed, the mourning of losses and the making of culture are synonymous activities. If we are to keep our lives flowing in a meaningful direction, we must become conscious of how the dead turn in their graves as we walk by over the top. Dialogue and communion are important. We must open ourselves to the questions and problems in which the souls of the dead are caught, for we only become fully-generative adults by taking on the burden of our forebear's karma. Mourning is not the process by means of which we let go of human beings. On the contrary, it is the *rite de passage* in which all generations join together to make human beings of one another.

Crucial to the mourning process, the process of imagining the culture of the dead, is updating the dead on our most contemporary discoveries. Indeed, we wrong our ancestors if we identify them with the letter of what they said and miss the spirit of it. Death does not mean closure. On the contrary, the dead continue to individuate their images through our imaginations. We must not think for a moment that death has sealed Freud into his *Collected Papers* as if into a narcissistic shell, or that Jung has become a Jungian. They are as busy as we are trying to absorb the teachings of Derrida and Lacan, Bateson and the others. In the timelessness of the imaginal psyche a huge symposium is being conducted, a symposium to which everyone is invited. There is Jung, talking to Plato. And over there is Tolstoy talking to my Uncle Fred. All souls who are on the same level of desire sit together, regardless of the their previous location in time and space.[3] Anachronism is a mode of recognition in elegy, a law of the imagination, the meeting place of angels. It is how "eternity" is experienced as an event of the soul.

REFERENCES

1. H. Corbin, Mundus Imaginalis or the Imaginary and the Imaginal, in *Spring: An Annual of Archetypal Psychology and Jungian Thought,* Spring Publication, Dallas, 1972.
2. R. Avens, *Imagination Is Reality,* Spring Publication, Dallas, 1980.
3. J. Hillman, *The Dream and the Underworld,* Harper & Row, New York, 1979.
4. W. H. Auden, *W. H. Auden: Collected Poems,* E. Mendelson (ed.), Random House, New York, 1976.
5. J. Hillman, *Archetypal Psychology: A Brief Account,* Spring Publications, Dallas, 1983.
6. P. B. Shelley, A Defense of Poetry, in *The Norton Anthology of English Literature,* (3rd Edition), M. H. Abrams et al., (eds.), W. W. Norton, New York, 1975.
7. R. Woodman, *The Apocalyptic Vision in the Poetry of Shelley,* Toronto University Press, Toronto, 1964.
8. J. Hillman, *Re-Visioning Psychology,* Harper & Row, New York, 1975.

[3] Here I follow Swedenborg: "Although all things appear in place and in space as they do in the world, still the angels have no notion or idea of place and space. [In fact,] all progressions in the spiritual world are effected by changes in the state of the interiors . . . Hence, those are near each other who are in a similar state, and those are far apart whose state is dissimilar . . ." [cited in 1].

CHAPTER 1

The Psychotherapy of the Dead: Loss and Character Structure in Freud's Metapsychology

LOSS

In 1923, in a slim volume titled *The Ego and the Id,* Freud articulated an idea of profound psychological value, an idea conversant with the ghostly presences which haunt our psychic life [1, p. 19].

> When it happens that a person has to give up a sexual object there quite often ensues an alteration of his ego which can only be described as a setting up of the object inside the ego . . .; the exact nature of this substitution is as yet unknown to us. It may be that by this introjection, which is a kind of regression to the mechanism of the oral phase, the ego makes it easier for the object to be given up or renders that process possible. It may be that this identification is the sole condition under which the id can give up its objects. At any rate the process, especially in the early phases of development, is a very frequent one, and it makes it possible to suppose that the character of the ego is a precipitate of abandoned object-cathexes and that it contains the history of those object-choices.

At first glance these sentences seem to contain little that Freud had not said earlier.[1] Indeed, the passage clearly alludes to the same

[1] Freud's 1910 study of Leonardo contains the first description of the mechanism whereby an object-cathexes is replaced by identification and introjection of the former object. In this paper Freud explains that one kind of homosexuality is the result of a boy identifying himself with his mother as a way to incorporate the loss which giving her up as a love-object has occasioned [2].

psychopathological processes which he reported on in his 1917 paper, "Mourning and Melancholia." There, too, the psyche's use of the mechanisms of introjection and identification when dealing with lost objects was discussed. What is important to understand about Freud's restatement in 1923 of an idea dating back to 1917 is that while the analysis of melancholia had been an end in itself in the early clinical paper, in the later, theoretical work it had become the *means* to something more ambitious. "At that time," writes Freud, referring to the early work on melancholia [1, p. 18]:

> . . . we did not appreciate the full significance of this process and did not know how common and how typical it is. Since then we have come to understand that this kind of substitution [i.e., the setting up in the ego of the lost object by means of identification] has a great share in determining the form taken by the ego and that it makes an essential contribution towards building up what is called 'character.'

While in "Mourning and Melancholia" Freud merely attempted to give a psychoanalytic account of depression, in *The Ego and the Id* he attempted to give a psychoanalytic account of the *structure* of the psyche itself. The later work describes the division of the mental apparatus into the institutions of ego, super-ego, and id, and it is in connection with the differentiation of these three structural entities that Freud recalls the mechanisms which are involved in mourning lost objects. Significantly, Freud writes that the specialization of the id into a tripartite system is the consequence of portions of the id having had to stand in for the very objects which the id has had to renounce. Ego and the super-ego, in other words, are formed from the id precisely in accordance with the hurts and losses the id has sustained during its travail in the external world [1, p. 38]:

> . . . we have said repeatedly that the ego is formed to a great extent out of identifications which take the place of abandoned cathexes by the id; that the first of these identifications always behave as a special agency in the ego and stand apart from the ego in the form of a super-ego. . . .

The *reflexive* psyche becomes a *reflective* psyche by recreating itself in the image and likeness of the object-cathexes it has had to abandon. A part of the id "assumes the features of the [absent] object" and "forcing itself . . . upon the id as a love-object [tries] to make good the id's loss by saying: 'Look, you can love me too—I am so like the object' " [1, p. 20]. As this process repeats itself again and again (now with this loss, now with that), "object libido" is gradually sublimated into "narcissistic libido" [1, p. 20], and a psychic life distinct from the world of outer objects, though not entirely divorced from it, becomes possible for the first time.

THE DEAD ZONE

Freud's account of how the id differentiates itself into a *reflective* psyche by identifying itself with the objects in the external world which it has lost bears a striking resemblance to his earlier speculations about how living matter first acquired sentient awareness and the rudiments of consciousness. In *Beyond the Pleasure Principle,* a book pre-dating its sequel—*The Ego and the Id*—by three years, Freud asks us to "picture a living organism in its most simplified possible form as an undifferentiated vesicle of a substance that is susceptible to stimulation" [3, p. 20]. Inasmuch as this organism interfaces with the external world, and inasmuch as its surfaces are altered by that contact, the relationship of its deeper layers to the surrounding environment will be a mediated one and an "organ for receiving stimuli" will have been established. "It would be easy to suppose," writes Freud [3, p. 20]:

> . . . that as a result of the ceaseless impact of external stimuli on the surface of the vesicle, its substance to a certain depth may have become permanently modified, so that excitatory processes run a different course in it from what they run in the deeper layers. A crust would thus be formed which would at last have been so thoroughly 'baked through' by stimulation that it would present the most favorable possible conditions for the reception of stimuli and become incapable of any further modification. In terms of the system *Cs.*, this would mean that its elements could undergo no further permanent modification from the passage of excitation, because they had already been modified in the respect in question to the greatest possible extent: now however, they would have become capable of giving rise to consciousness.

This account of the development of sentient awareness in living matter is the background against which Freud's ideas about the development of reflective centers in the reflexive id must be read. To fully grasp the metapsychological dimension of Freud's idea about the internalization of lost objects we must appreciate that this process is not restricted merely to clinically defined entities such as grief, depression, and the Oedipus-complex, but figures as well in the life of "the living organism in its most simplified possible form." Just as portions of the id identify themselves with those aspects of the external world with which the id cannot maintain object-relations, the outer surface of the simplest life form "becomes to some degree inorganic and thenceforward functions as a special envelope or membrane resistant to stimuli" [3, p. 21]. As Freud writes in *The Ego and the Id* [1, p. 15]:

> . . . the ego is that part of the id which has been modified by the direct influence of the external world . . .; in a sense it is an extension of the surface-differentiation. Moreover, the ego seeks to bring the influence of the external world to bear upon the id and its tendencies, and endeavors to substitute the reality principle for the pleasure principle which reigns unrestrictedly in the id.

Like the surface of the simple vesicle which returns to the inorganic state and forms a crust around the deeper living layers, the id insulates itself behind the ego—that part of itself that has been "modified by the direct influence of the external world."

Now the crucial thing to grasp here is that the ego, no less than the outer surface of the simple vesicle, is largely dead—'a precipitate of abandoned object-cathexes . . . [which] contains the history of those object-choices" [1, p. 19]. Indeed, what Freud wrote about the dead layer of the simple vesicle could be said as well of the layer of introjected dead objects which differentiate the id into a reflective system of interacting institutions (id, ego, and super-ego) and cast the die in which the ego's "character" is set [3, p. 21]:

> By its death, the outer layer has saved all the deeper ones from a similar fate—unless, that is to say, stimuli reach it which are so strong that they break through the protective shield. *Protection against* stimuli is an almost more important function for the living organism than *reception of* stimuli. . . . The main purpose of the *reception* of stimuli is to discover the direction and nature of the external stimuli; and for that it is enough to take small specimens of the external world, to sample it in small quantities.

When we analyze the *character* of the ego we discover that it functions in precisely this way. The unmourned libidinal losses which the psyche has denied form a dead zone around the deeper libidinal trends making them invulnerable to similar hurts. Gradually, *rigor mortis* sets in. The identifications which have been made with lost love-objects stiffen into fixed attitudes. Love-lorn desires, desires which have been spurned, betrayed, let down or killed by their encounter with the external world, form themselves into a narcissistic shell, thereby saving the rest of the psyche from a similar fate. One by one, corpses pile up in the mind until finally that distinctive blend of "protection against stimuli" and "reception of stimuli," which psychology calls "character structure," emerges.

RESISTANCE AND THE THIRD *UCS*

In therapy, character structure expresses itself as *resistance.* When the patient is asked to free-associate, answer a question, or complete a task, his performance is frequently hindered by inner obstacles. At certain points during the session the patient "draws a blank," fumbles with his words, suddenly changes the topic, or denies that his tears mean anything. At these moments the therapist is left with the impression that the patient has stumbled over something in himself which he cannot see—the unmourned corpse of an abandoned love-object, perhaps.

In Freud's view, these resistant behaviors and lapses in performance indicate the presence of unconscious elements *within* the ego itself [1, p. 7]:

> . . . we find during analysis that, when we put certain tasks before the patient, he gets into difficulties; his associations fail when they should be coming near the repressed. We then tell him that he is dominated by a resistance; but he is quite unaware of the fact, and, even if he guesses from his unpleasurable feelings that a resistance is now at work in him, he does not know what it is or how to describe it. Since, however, there can be no question but that this resistance emanates from his ego and belongs to it, we find ourselves in an unforeseen situation. We have come upon something in the ego itself which is also unconscious, which behaves exactly like the repressed—that is, which produces powerful effects without itself being conscious and which requires special work before it can be made conscious.

Freud's clinical observation that "resistance emanates from the [patient's] ego and belongs to it" was an observation with vast metapsychological implications. The presence of dead zones or blind spots within the ego itself suggested to Freud the need to re-vision his previous conception of the mind, a conception which explained, among other things, neurosis as the result of a conflict between the conscious and unconscious minds.

Previously, the clinical phenomena upon which the theory of the unconscious was based could all be shown to have once been conscious, and the term unconscious, therefore, implied a *repressed* unconscious. With the discovery, however, of unconscious areas in the ego, *areas which had never been conscious,* Freud found it necessary to posit in addition to the repressed unconscious and the preconscious "a third *Ucs.*, which is not repressed . . ." [1, p. 8].

In order to understand what Freud had in mind when positing this "third *Ucs.*" it is necessary to look back once more to his description, in *Beyond the Pleasure Principle,* of the development of sentient awareness in the simple vesicle. The unconscious areas in the ego which manifest themselves in therapy as resistance correspond to the outer surface of the simple vesicle, a surface which has "[become] to some degree inorganic and [which] thenceforward functions as a special envelope or membrane resistant to stimuli" [3, p. 21]. Like this other surface, permanently altered by the external world, the areas of the ego which have been hardened into character by hurt and loss constitute the filtering system which the ego requires in order to "become capable of giving rise to consciousness" [3, p. 21].

Resistance, in other words, is an incredibly subtle phenomenon "arising from the same higher strata and systems of the mind which originally carried out repression" [3, p. 13]. Though it impedes the insight which the therapeutic process works toward, as the "protective shield against stimuli" it is also the mediating factor which has made consciousness possible in the first place.

If it were not for the resistances which constitute the third unconscious, the analysis of the repressed unconscious would be a relatively simple matter. After all, the 'repressed' want nothing more than to break into consciousness or to discharge themselves in action [3, p. 13]. But just at the moment when an interpretation would bring them into awareness, they get stuck in the resistant filter to which awareness owes its being. The patient, with a shake of his head, declares that the interpretation does not "click." It is not that the patient is willfully refusing to cooperate; rather, it is that the character structure of his consciousness is getting in the way. Inside its protective shell of wounded narcissism, the patient's ego, that "precipitate of abandoned object-cathexes [which] contains the history of those object-choices" [1, p. 19], is unable to incorporate the repressed despite their willingness to be absorbed. The more the therapist tries to bring the repressed contents into awareness the more clearly the dead zone within the patient's ego displays itself by thwarting him in his efforts. At this point the treatment must leave to one side the analysis of the repressed unconscious and address the ways in which the patient's consciousness is hardened against itself.

ABSENCE AND PRESENCE

The perceptual categories of the conscious mind are a function of the identifications which the id has made with its lost objects. Just as the ego is a "precipitate of abandoned object-cathexes . . ." [1, p. 19], ego-*consciousness* is a precipitate composed of the small quantities of stimuli which have been able to filter through this dead zone of identifications which Freud called the "third *Ucs.*"

It is not simply that "perception plays [for the ego] the part which in the id falls to instinct" [1, p. 15]; in a deeper sense, *perception is derived from the instincts even as the ego is derived from the id.* Every act of perception is pre-dated by the partial petrification of an earlier instinctual trend. Portions of the id, having likened themselves to the love-objects which the id has lost or renounced, create a multitude of protective "shields against stimuli," shields which enable the deeper layers of the psyche to sample the external world in "small quantities."

It is as if the id's blind, spasming passions had created from the wreck of their own hope the very objects they had sought cathexes with. "Even after my skin is destroyed, Yet from my flesh I shall see God" (Job 19:26). Like Job, abandoned by God and bedeviled with boils, the reflective psyche's capacity "to see" develops in accordance with the ways in which the id has been destroyed by it lost objects. So long as the loss of an object results in an alteration in the outer surfaces of an instinctual life-form, the "object" will become—*in its absence*—the category by means of which that life-form perceives.

The absent object, precisely by virtue of being absent, is no longer *what* we see but *how* we see.[2] Perception is a nostalgic phenomenon; there is a longing in it, a longing which causes us to see what's "out there" in terms of what is no longer "out there" at all.

[2] I allude here to Edward Casey's statement: "The image is not *what* is present to awareness—this is the content proper—but *how* this content is presented" [4, p. 10].

The ways we have been spurned, betrayed, abandoned and killed by objects, both phylogenetically and ontogenetically, determine the ways in which our perceptual system construes all subsequent events. Everything we see is filtered through the apertures of dead love. Everything we see, we see through the eyes of the dead. The psyche is an *afterworld* of love.

If, as Blake put it, "a World [can be glimpsed] in a Grain of Sand, And a Heaven in a Wild Flower," it is precisely because the psyche, having lost its objects, imagines through spectacles which have been tinted by that loss. No matter where he looks—at a flower, a grain of sand, or the analyst—the patient, like the poet, "sees" the objects he has internalized. All perception, in other words, is a function of transference. The losses with which the psyche has identified function as the beam through which the mote in brother's eye is seen. Nothing can escape the cataracts of loss. Nothing can be heard in a new way. The signifiers have become identical with the objects they once signified. Even interpretations that are carefully worded to bring this problem into awareness are immediately construed by the patient into experiences which confirm his constant attitude. Unable to see *how* he sees, the patient remains imprisoned in the hell of trying to retain a living connection to the dead by projecting their images onto others in subsequent relationships.

Perception, like mourning, is a melancholy business *grounded in the identification of bereaved instincts with objects whose loss they cannot grieve*. It is not simply that we see our dead loved ones in visions after they have left us; the dearly departed are the seat of the visioning faculty itself. Their unsung ghosts, lingering on in the cemetery of the "third *Ucs.*," are the invisible medium through which we see.

THE CHARACTER OF CONSCIOUSNESS

Who we are is largely a function of how each day we have died a little. Like other living creatures, it is not the pink tissues of our inner life which give us our specific definition and form, but the composition of our exterior surfaces. Just as we recognize a turtle from its shell and a rhinoceros from its hide, the character of a personality is discernible in the ways in which it has been hardened by its contact with the external world. Character structure is that part of the personality which has been modified by the external world to the greatest possible extent, and which is no longer capable of further modification. It is that once-passionate part of us which has returned to a state resembling that of objects in the external world with which our passions have lost connection.

From its very beginning, life is a deathly process through which each of us becomes precisely those things we have died seeking. Petrified in nostalgic postures, our aim-inhibited instincts transform themselves into modes of consciousness which construe all objects as if they were the object we have lost.

Of course, at first this transformation of object-libido into narcissistic-libido plays an important role for the psyche as a whole. Indeed, without the defensive maneuver of converting absent objects into inner objects the libidinal-soul could well be annihilated by its hurts and losses. This is especially true when we are young and our inventory of remembered experiences is not large enough to provide a sufficient field of comparison through which to relativize the vicissitudes we suffer. At times such as these, times when we lack the perspective previous experiences provide, identification is a saving grace.

With the passage of time, however, the negative effects of our unconscious identifications begin to out-balance the earlier, beneficial effects. Gaps widen between the character structure we developed to face the trials of an earlier time and the trials which face us in the present moment. Living out each day as if it were the eternal recurrence of some yesterday we could not grieve, our fundamental adaptation to life gradually becomes more and more antiquated until, at last, we ourselves become outmoded.

While it is true that to the analyst this rootedness of the personality in character defenses feels like "resistance," the term is ill-chosen. Do we call the turtle resistant because the way it has adapted itself to the external world in the course of its evolution has not equipped it to fly? What psychoanalysis calls resistance might better be understood as the inevitable consequences of the unconscious underpinnings (unconscious in the sense of the "third *Ucs.*") of consciousness. The losses with which we identify and which form the barrier against stimuli, which is also the threshold of consciousness, each orient awareness in their own specific terms. To be conscious in one way is simultaneously to be unconscious in another and vice versa. Though the calloused fingers of the guitarist may adapt him to the making of music, they are a liability for the reading of braille.

How do we become conscious of the ways we are conscious, the ways in which we are *dead* conscious? How do we become conscious of the identifications with the dead which have made consciousness possible and which define its acuity and limit its vision? So long as consciousness does not know what it is standing in for, it is without insight into its own stance. How does the *reflective* psyche become aware of its generative connection to the *reflexive* psyche and so become *self*-reflective?

Gaining insight into the specific absence which is at any given moment serving as the seat of consciousness is a process identical with the amputee's recognition that the pained limb which he feels beneath the flat sheet of his hospital bed is a *phantom* limb. Consciousness, like the occult sensations which animate the space where a limb once twitched, is the phantom form of an amputated instinctual trend.

It is not that defenses are mobilized by the ego to protect consciousness from hurt and loss; consciousness itself is called into being as a defense against hurt and loss. Just as every act of perception, according to the spirit if not the letter of Freud's metapsychological account, is an attempt by a specialized portion of the id to stand in for a lost object, the mandate of consciousness is principally one of defense. We are abandoned to consciousness and hurt into awareness precisely to the extent of our ability to deny our hurts and losses. Even when consciousness seems to be cognizant of hurt and pain, the flamboyant character of this awareness may be its way of keeping itself from directly facing the actual proportions of the scene of loss to which it owes its origin. Reflective awareness, in other words, is a reaction formation to specific object-losses. Like the patient who denies the loss of a limb or the mother who denies the death of a child, consciousness is the result of attempts by the mental apparatus to proceed *as if* it had not lost the love-objects of its instinctual life.

The model in terms of which we are here imagining consciousness is the same model Freud used to elucidate the pathological condition of melancholia: mourning. If consciousness is to gain insight into itself it must mourn the dead objects and petrified instincts of which its existence is but a precipitate.

There is a way of seeing that is simultaneously a way of grieving. Wherever attention is directed, full recognition is granted to the transience of all things. Eliot saw in this manner when he described "April" as the "cruelest month," and Keats did as well when he wrote of "April" as a "shroud." Upon closer scrutiny, the mode of consciousness we are describing here not only recognizes that the objects it perceives are fleeting, but that it owes them a debt. Everything that dies is an ancestor of consciousness, deserving of ancestor worship. And nothing is fully a *content* of consciousness until the *style* of awareness which consciousness has adopted in denial of its loss is fitted with a mourner's band. Elegiac consciousness is a mode of awareness which can represent at one and the same moment that pathos of the libido which has survived an object's loss and the object which was lost. Encouraged to grieve, ego-consciousness need no longer "rage against the dying of the light," performing necrophilia in the name of transference with whatever it encounters. The dead which have been left to be buried by the dead must be exhumed from the blind spot of ego-consciousness and given proper burial.

EXHUMING THE CORPSES

In order to care for the psyche, psychotherapy must care for the dead. Like a homicide detective, a forensic scientist, an undertaker or a priest, the therapist must assist the patient in identifying the lost objects and decomposing instincts which the therapy hours have turned up, and ensure that they are provided with a proper burial. The skeletons in the family closet, the aborted fetuses of infantile desire, the corpse in the trunk of the abandoned car: each body must be exhumed from the makeshift grave of the patient's character structure, named, washed, embalmed, viewed in an open casket, and laid to rest beside its next of kin.

Psychotherapy can be a grisly business. When the work begins to touch upon the patient's character structure, dreams and fantasies of a macabre nature are not uncommon. The heads of family members may roll through eerie hallways. The dream-ego may try repeatedly to hide a corpse only to have it discovered again by playing children. A dream series may develop in which the dream-ego implements ever more drastic solutions to the problem of destroying the bodies of the dead. Explosives may be detonated, bodies dissolved in a corrosive acid—all to no avail.

Analyzing a patient's constant attitude can be like interrogating a serial killer. It is seldom enough to extract a confession from a single resistance. Indeed, disclosures which the patient makes while under the duress of questioning may be merely of the pleading-guilty-to-a-lesser-crime variety. The patient is usually all too willing to confess the secondary gains which have been the perks of his neurosis. The therapist must remember, however, that the character structure of the ego is inherently psychopathic, a precipitate of the objects which his id has lost or killed. The bodies of the dead are seldom hidden exactly where the patient says they are, for he has preserved them in his *style* of confessing their whereabouts. His character is their illicit graveyard even as their deaths have made him who he is. If, at the next session, the therapist is surprised to be still pulling teeth, it is likely that in the last session he was seduced by disclosure and thrown off the trail [5, p. 173]. As the psychoanalyst Roy Schafer has written, it is not the content which the resistance seems to be repressing that is important, but the resistance itself.[3] Each instance of resistance is a hidden body which therapy must help the patient to face. Only by facilitating a mourning process can the psychopathic resistances which underpin the patient's constant attitude be worked through.

Since the way patients attempt to maintain a living connection to the therapist is a reaction formation to the loss of other significant relationships, transference phenomena are of particular importance in the therapy of the dead. At this point it is not the projection which the patient places onto the therapist that is of crucial importance so much as the way the patient resists acknowledging that the relationship is being dominated by a projection. In order to see through his projections, the patient must be able to grieve. Rigid characters develop rigid transferences, because they would rather exploit the therapeutic relationship as a replacement for old losses than use the occasion, as the therapist would prefer, to mourn the dead. Again, the patient might pretend to see through his projections if that is what he thinks he must do to keep the therapist cast in the object relationship of the past, whose loss he has been unable to face.

When the therapist understands that his struggle with a patient's character structure is a struggle with a mourning process which has been indefinitely postponed, he will be able to perform his priestly functions. It is simply not enough to adopt the secular posture of the classical psychoanalyst and analyze the transference as if it contained nothing more that the infantilisms of an immature man or woman. Though, it is true, many of the losses which the patient has impersonated (identification) in order to deny their passing were sustained in childhood, treating them as vulgar impulses in need of sublimation misses the point. Anachronistic behavior is merely a consequence of the failure of the patient to mourn losses. Admonishing the patient to "grow-up" merely preserves the identification. Indeed, "growing up"

[3] "Instead of succumbing to the analysand's seduction by disclosure, the analyst should bring the analysand back to the prior question about the difficult moment and underline the importance of understanding it fully" [5, p. 173].

can only occur to the extent that the patient can give up the various selves that maturation requires he leave behind.

In his priestly role, the therapist's task is to facilitate whatever grieving processes the patient has deferred. The patient must be helped to *imagine* his losses as opposed to literally being them. Identification and introjection are failures of representation. The patient ceases to be a personality and becomes a more or less rigid character to the extent that he can no longer imagine a difference between himself and the losses he has experienced. As characters, we are made in the image and likeness of whatever events we have been unable to imagine. Grieving is essentially an imaginal process. We pore over old photographs, hold conversations with departed dear ones, acquaint ourselves with the topography of the afterworld of our religious tradition, and worry whether our loved ones are at rest in the beyond. The purpose of psychotherapy, or at least of an analytic psychotherapy, is to embody our absent objects in the cultural imagination.

BURYING THE DEAD

Different peoples bury their dead in different ways. In some cultures the dead are buried in the earth, in others they are consumed with flames. Some peoples submerge the deceased in rivers and seas, and others place them on high racks to be consumed by birds. Earth, fire, water, air: each elemental mode of corporeal disintegration has a corresponding funerary practice built around it, as if a virtue were being made of a necessity. Earth to earth, ashes to ashes, dust to dust: by going with the decay, by anticipating and facilitating the disintegrative process through one of the various funerary modes, man presides over the ultimate removal of himself from bodily life and so conquers death.

The body, being mortal and having died subject to natural causes, *must be prevented from being subjected to nature a second time.* If man can be said to possess an immortal soul it can be so only to the extent that he has made of himself something which is beyond nature. By subverting the natural process of decay (whether by speeding it up or slowing it down), what is unnatural or extra-natural in the person of the dead is spared, at least on the symbolic level, the defilement which the natural process of decay would spell for it.

Freud, in *Beyond the Pleasure Principle,* writes of the ego's attempts to master the aversive situations of which it is the passive recipient by actively promoting them [3, p. 10]. The idea came to him while observing his young grandson mastering the anxiety of being briefly separated from his mother. By throwing a ball out of sight with the word "*f-o-o-ort*" ("gone") and then retrieving it by the string to which it was attached with the word "*Da*" ("there"), the boy mastered in play the object-loss of which he was the passive recipient. Doubtless, a similar action underpins funerary practices. The survivors, like Freud's little grandson, comfort themselves, on some primitive level, with the idea that what *they* have placed in the beyond *they* can also retrieve or be re-united with.

But it is important not to apply this notion of ego-mastery too reductively. While funerary rituals do help relatives and friends of the deceased to come to terms with object-loss, their most important purpose is the care of the dead. Death is not merely a problem for the living. It poses difficulties for the dead as well. In as much as a person has made of himself or herself something more than nature, nature's naked elements will prove an unsuitable grave. Think of our dreams and fantasies: none of the "material" modes in which we attempt to bury the dead is sufficient to the task. Bodies buried one day come back to life the next. Ghosts linger on for years, rattling the chains of desire which bind them to the living. A new-born child may be named for a dead sibling, forestalling both its own psychological birth and the passover of the dead child's soul into its final resting place.

Despite the ritualistic attention afforded to the material modes of burial, it is not in earth, air, fire or water that the dead receive their proper burial, so much as it is in the ancestors. We do not bury the dead in the elements, *we bury them in the dead.* Others have gone before us. The earth in which we will be buried, the fire in which we will be cremated, the water in which we will be dissolved, and the air in which we will be dispersed are already densely populated. The elements are all *subtle* elements, *modes of the imagination.*

Nature gives way to culture only when its elements have been sufficiently saturated with death. The history of man properly begins in that moment when it makes sense to say that the earth is buried in the dead. What Freud believed made consciousness possible is precisely what makes culture possible as well. Those that have preceded us into the grave have created, through their deaths, a protective shield against stimuli which is simultaneously a threshold of consciousness. As Lacan has put it, ". . . Empedocles, by throwing himself into Mount Etna, leaves forever present in the memory of men this symbolic act of his being-for-death" [6, p. 84].

Man can inhabit nothing psychologically until he has lost it or been killed by it. Outer space, for instance, is still largely an impersonal void. Though we have walked on the moon, sent satellites into orbit, and lived for sustained periods in space stations, space still feels inhuman and soulless. It all seems just a clever trick until the spaceship explodes and that huge immensity of space becomes contained in the cancelled bodies of our dead astronauts. It was not with the moon-walk that man entered the space age so much as when the space shuttle, Challenger, manned with men and women representing several races, exploded those few seconds after launching before a worldwide television audience.[4]

Patients with rigid character structures, patients who impersonate their losses rather than imagining by means of them, must be reminded of the collective losses which have become the constituting structures of world culture. Just as in the *Meno* Socrates leads the slave-boy to recollect knowledge he did not know he had, the therapist must acquaint the patient with the symbolic order (Lacan) or collective unconscious (Jung), that realm of cancelled objects which have preceded him into the grave and which now wait to receive and eternalize the desires which have ensouled his grievous losses.

After free-association (or, rather, the failure of free-association) has led us to the specific corpse, elucidation through comparison with cultural parallels—Jung's technique of amplification—may provide the route to burial. When the patient's constant attitude is amplified by its cultural prototypes, the patient can begin to individuate himself out from his various identifications. Like Shelley after he buried Keats in the cultural imagination with the writing of *Adonais,* the patient who has been linked through loss to culture need no longer "vex, with inharmonious sighs/ The silence of that heart's accepted sacrifice" [7, p. 1797].

The cultural imagination, that realm of objects which have lost their signified life and become in their absence modes of signification, provides our losses a place to go. When I watch Lear weeping over the body of Cordelia, I too can weep for the corpses which structure my own constant attitude. And when I watch Oedipus put out his eyes with the brooch pins of the dead Jocasta, I, too, can begin to see the Oedipal blinkers through which I have been perceiving. Character on the stage is character in the right place. Aristotle is to the Freudian point: Tragedy is cathartic. Seated in the audience, I am, through my participating emotions, part of the action, and as the stories

[4] I am indebted to Prof. Ross Woodman for this illustration.

individuate their characters and advance their plots, my identifications are individuated as well. When the curtain falls, the tragedy of identification that I could not finish myself may have also reached its close. The house lights are turned back on; Hades fades away. Liberated from their roles, the actors return to the stage to receive the applause. Leaving the theater after the performance, the patient himself need no longer perform the part assigned him by the losses he could not grieve. Indeed, he may no longer be a "patient" at all, but rather, a patron of that subtlest playwright, Death itself.

REFERENCES

1. S. Freud, *The Ego and the Id,* J. Riviere (trans.), J. Strachey (ed.), W. W. Norton, New York, 1962.
2. S. Freud, Leonardo da Vinci and a Memory of His Childhood" (1910), *Standard Edition of the Complete Psychological Works of Sigmund Freud,* Vol. XI, J. Strachey (ed.), Hogarth Press and The Institute of Psychoanalysis, London, 1953-1974.
3. S. Freud, *Beyond the Pleasure Principle,* S. Strachey (ed.), W. W. Norton, New York, 1961.
4. E. Casey, Toward a Phenomenology of Imagination, *The Journal of the British Society of Phenomenology,* Vol. 5, 1974.
5. R. Schafer, *The Analytic Attitude,* Basic Books, New York, 1983.
6. J. Lacan, *The Language of the Self: The Function of Language in Psychoanalysis,* A. Wilden (trans.), Dell Publishing, New York, 1968.
7. P. B. Shelley, *Adonais,* in *The Norton Anthology of English Literature,* (3rd Edition), M. H. Abrams et al. (eds.), W. W. Norton, New York, 1975.

10.20

CHAPTER 2

Irreplaceable Objects: An Imaginal Approach to the Mourning of Inconsolable Losses

Not marble, nor the gilded monuments
Of princes, shall outlive this powerful rhyme;
But you shall shine more bright in these contents
Than unswept stone, besmeared with sluttish time.
When wastful war shall statues overturn,
And broils root out the work of masonry,
Nor Mars his sword nor war's quick fire shall burn
The living record of your memory.
'Gainst death and all-oblivious enmity
Shall you pace forth; your praise shall still find room
Even in the eyes of all posterity
That wear this world out to the ending doom.
So, till the judgement that yourself arise,
You live in this, and dwell in lover's eyes [1, pp. 479-480].

William Shakespeare

IMAGINAL OBJECTS

The inner experiences which constitute the content of the mourning process bear witness to the irreplaceability of our lost objects. The dead friend who no longer visits, the dead parent who no longer calls, and the dead spouse who no longer warms the bed beside us persist in the imagination with an unprecedented vividness. Viewed from the "inside," mourning is as much the beginning of an imaginal relationship as it is the ending of a material one. The unconscious, as Freud said, cannot represent negation [2, p. 353]. The same voice that announces the death of a dear one calls into being a personified category of the imagination as well. Although our loved ones are "gone" they are also "not gone."

The specific *pathos* which characterizes mourning is a function of this paradoxical relationship between absence and presence. Although the inner images which continue the existence of the lost object in the mind may be as sweet as the acceptance of the absence of the outer object is bitter, the two do not belie one another. Indeed, we reconcile ourselves to the one reality only to the extent that we have reconciled ourselves to the other. Like two locked boxes each containing the other's key, death (object loss) and the imagination unlock each other's mysteries.

Of course, if it were simply that the dead appear in the mind as they had appeared to our senses while still alive, we could discount their importance. Indeed, if they were nothing more than memory images, reaching out to them in the imagination would be a category error similar to that made by the bereaved when they reach across the bed to embrace a spouse who is no longer there. But the figures which animate bereavement, though similar to the persons who once animated our lives, manifest themselves in a fashion distinct from their previous existence. We are surprised by what they say and do. We see them as we never saw them before. Being dead, they are now no longer attenuated by what we had required them to be and may now appear as they actually are.

It is not just that "we don't know what we've got till it's gone." The corollary is also true. Losing an object is the psyche's way of finding it. By becoming absent an object becomes wholly psychological. By losing life it gains the eternal life of the imaginal psyche. It becomes a subtle body, an imaginal object, an image, an angel.

In bereavement, the ontological assumptions which tell us that our loved ones no longer exist are shaken by the ontological assumptions through which these absent objects, now imaginal objects, persist. Suddenly we realize that we have buried them alive in our materialistic assumptions about what constitutes reality. Suddenly we realize that we have *always* buried them in our materialistic assumptions about what is ontologically real. But now, perhaps for the first time, we begin to appreciate their value. They are denizens of the permanent mind. Where once we saw them imperfectly through the dark glass of our own projections, we now can see the faces they wore before they were born.

FREUD'S BIAS

In answer to the question—"in what consists the work which mourning performs?"—Freud writes [3, p. 154]:

> The testing of reality, having shown that the loved object no longer exists, requires forthwith that all the libido shall be withdrawn from its attachments to this object. Against this demand a struggle of course arises—it may be universally observed that man never willingly abandons a libido-position, not even when a substitute is already beckoning to him. This struggle can be so intense that a turning away from reality ensues, the object being clung to through the medium of a hallucinatory wish-psychosis. The normal outcome is that deference for reality gains the day. Nevertheless its behest cannot be at once obeyed. The task in now carried through bit by bit, under great expense of time and cathectic energy, while all the time the existence of the lost object is continued in the mind. Each single one of the memories and hopes which bound the libido to the object is brought up and hyper-cathected, and the detachment of the libido from it is accomplished. Why this process of carrying out the behest of reality bit by bit, which is in the nature of a compromise, should be so extraordinarily painful is not at all easy to explain in terms of mental economics. It is worth noting that the pain seems natural to us. The fact is, however, that when the work of mourning is completed the ego becomes free and uninhibited again.

This account of the work of mourning, an account which underpins much of the subsequent research on the mourning process, is based on a materialistic bias. For Freud, mourning is a fixation of libido to objects which no longer exist, a fixation which painfully resists, but sooner or latter succumbs, to the reality principle. Although he does not view mourning as a pathological syndrome, he speaks of it, nevertheless, as if it were. Mourning implies a "turning away from reality." The lost object is being "clung to through the medium of a hallucinatory wish-psychosis." The process is said to make great demands on "time and cathectic energy."

There is something soulless about Freud's account of this most soulful of processes. Although he sensitively portrays something of the pain of mourning, he is wholly insensitive to the lasting value of the lost object. Mourning, in Freud's account, consists of little more than the breaking of the habits associated with the object, habits which continue to bind us to the object despite the fact that the object is gone.

Freud's blind spot here is a consequence of his viewing the lost object exclusively from the standpoint of drive theory. Since the object no longer affords an avenue to the reduction of the drives, it must be replaced by a more suitable one. From this perspective, the pain of mourning is merely the pain of withdrawal. Though "man never willing abandons a libido-position, not even when a substitute is already beckoning to him," "deference for reality gains the day" when repeated attempts to gain satisfaction from the absent object, as its existence is "continued in the mind," fail. Like an addict recovering from an addiction, the ego recovers from its lost object.

But does the drive-theory account of mourning do justice to our experience of loss? Are our dead friends and relatives nothing more than lost objects? Is there nothing unique in our loss? Are the dead as replaceable as drive theory maintains? Should we really go out on another blind date when we are only now beginning to see what the dead mean to us?

Perhaps, Freud's difficulty in "explain[ing] [mourning] in terms of mental economics" resides in the fact that instinctual drives are not the only currency in which the process trades. The fact that a portion of libido remains committed to an object long after that object has ceased to exist in the world of "really real reality" may mean that something else is going on. Perhaps, the energy is changing its form and being utilized in another way. Perhaps, the bereaved widow brooding over the image of her dead husband is making him into a part of her inner life, a part of her soul. Present now precisely through his absence, the dead man initiates her into the *ontology* of loss. She sees him in dreams, standing beside her dead father,-smiling. From the point of view of "reality," of course, her husband has become extinct. From the point of view of the imagination, however, he is now eternal. Bit by bit, the eros, as Hillman has said, "is getting psychized" [4, p. 180]. The very man with whom she once explored life, or rather, his imago, is now initiating her into the imaginal.

Of course, the inner world of mourning need not be seen as conflicting with the establishment of new outer relationships. In fact, when relationships to the dead are maintained it makes it less likely that their images will be reincarnated in the form of projections which distort our relationships with other people. A particularized awareness of the dead is necessary if there is to be a particularized awareness of the individual uniqueness of the living. A heart that grieves, a heart that communes with the dead in reverie, is immune to falling in love on the rebound. By welcoming the ghosts the bereaved may find themselves to be no longer haunted by them.

Despite the materialistic bias which characterizes Freud's analysis of mourning, in letters to bereaved friends and colleagues he displayed a more compassionate understanding of the process. Indeed, in a letter of condolence written to Ludwig Binswanger, Freud supplemented his ideas about mourning in a fashion that shows that he was not unaware of the value of the nostalgic tie to the dead which the bereaved may wish to cultivate [5, p. 386]:

> Although we know that after such a loss the acute state of mourning will subside, we also know we shall remain inconsolable and will never find a substitute. No matter what may fill the gap, even if it be filled completely, it nevertheless remains something else. And actually this is how it should be. It is the only way of perpetuating that love which we do not want to relinquish.

MOURNING AS SOUL-MAKING

> Peace, peace! he is not dead, he doth not sleep—
> He hath awakened from the dream of life—
> 'Tis we, who lost in stormy visions, keep
> With phantoms an unprofitable strife,
> And in mad trance, strike with our spirit's knife
> Invulnerable nothings.—*We* decay
> Like corpses in a charnel; fear and grief
> Convulse us and consume us day by day,
> And cold hopes swarm like worms within our living clay [1, p. 1798].

This stanza from Shelley's poem, *Adonais*, is not a denial of the death of Keats. Shelley, in writing this verse, is not enacting the mourning process as Freud described it in "Mourning and Melancholia." His assertion, "Peace, peace! he is not dead . . . ," cannot be read as clinical evidence that Shelley is clinging to Keats through the medium of a "hallucinatory wish-psychosis." On the contrary, the elegy is Shelley's attempt to bury Keats in the cultural imagination. The mourning process enacted in the poem is closer to the account of the process Freud gives in his letter to Binswanger: "Although we know that after such a loss the acute state of mourning will subside, we also know we shall remain inconsolable and will never find a substitute." The images of the poem resolve the "acute stage of mourning" not by denying the loss or by replacing it, but by precisely imagining Keats' irreplaceable uniqueness. To the extent that Shelley is able to absorb the emotion stirred by Keats' death into images, he need not "vex, with inharmonious sighs/The silence of that heart's accepted sacrifice" [1, p. 1797].

In *Adonais* Shelley is not detaching his "memories and expectations . . . from the dead."[1] Nor is he auditioning others to take the place of Keats in the world's affections. Such moves as these would constitute the soul's *un*making. Rather, Shelley is gathering the young poet to his own images, locating him amongst the fellowship of the dead, making him into soul. Keats, we are told, is now "a portion of the loveliness/ Which once he made more lovely . . ." [1, p. 1799]. In verse 14 a wake is imagined in which "All he had loved, and moulded into thought/ Form shape, and hue, and odour and sweet sound,/Lament" him [1, p. 1792]. And in verses 45 and 46 Shelley imagines Keats entering the company of other young poets who died before achieving the fame that was their due. "Robed in dazzling immortality" these "inheritors of unfulfilled renown," cry out to Keats, "Assume thy winged throne, thou Vesper of our throng!" [1, p. 1800].

Though this may not be as science would have it, it is, as Freud comments in his letter to Binswanger, "as it should be." With the writing of *Adonais*, Shelley created a vehicle capable of perpetuating that love for Keats which the world does "not want to relinquish" [1, p. 1799].

> He has outsoared the shadow of our night;
> Envy and calumny and hate and pain,
> And that unrest which men miscall delight,
> Can touch him not and torture not again;
> From the contagion of the world's slow stain;
> He is secure, and now can never mourn
> A heart grown cold, a head grown grey in vain;
> Nor, when the spirit's self has ceased to burn,
> With sparkless ashes load an unlamented urn.

While it is entirely fitting that Keats, the poet who coined the term "Soul-making," should be perpetuated beyond his death in the subtle body which Shelley's elegy provides him, it would be a mistake to think that any of us may not mourn in a similarly poetic genre. True, we may not be strong poets, and our dead may not have been "mourning star[s] among the living" [1, p. 1788], but if their loss is as irreplaceable for us

[1] Freud writes: "Mourning has a very distinct psychic task to perform, namely, to detach the memories and expectations of the survivors from the dead" [6, p. 858].

as the cultural loss of Keats was for Shelley, we too will have to relate in imagination to those loved ones whom our hearts cannot relinquish. In a word, the poets speak for us.

INTERNALIZING THE IRREPLACEABLE

When "death does us part," the "for better or for worse" which constituted our life with the deceased may at first seem dead as well. The period of depression that follows the loss of a significant relationship devastates the identity of the survivor. Indeed, to the extent that we are disconnected from the deceased we are also disconnected from ourselves.

Patient: I feel like a zombie. I was at a party last evening, but I was not really myself. Without Elizabeth to laugh at my jokes, I no longer seem to have a sense of Humor. I could always see life's ironies with her.

Therapist: You miss the laughter. You find that your sense of humor is cancelled out by her death.

Patient: Who is it who died—Elizabeth or me? It's like without her I have no soul.

Therapist: You cannot get in touch with that particular part of yourself which she touched?

Patient: Yeah, you know, I had always thought of myself as being my own person. I hadn't realized how much I was me through her.

Therapist: Is that bad?

Patient: No, just surprising. I suppose that all my friends bring out different sides of me. It's just that the side of me and the side of life which Elizabeth connected me to is gone.

Therapist: Strange, that now, in her absence, you are learning so much about her and about yourself.

Patient: How's that?

Therapist: Well it's like that meditation of John Donne's. It is precisely because "no man is an island" that the bell that tolls for anybody also tolls for you.

Patient: Elizabeth would like that.

Therapist: Do *you* like that?

Patient: Yes.

Therapist: So there you are yourself again, enjoying the ironies.
Patient: Hello, Elizabeth.

As the outer persons die, the inner world becomes more densely populated and a discipline for connecting to them becomes imperative. With each loss the imagination becomes the place we live from precisely as we once had lived through others. They are there, backing our reflections, informing our perceptions, guaranteeing us continuity of self in a world convulsed with change. And although we may now be more consciously aware of how these others are us, they are also not us. We can still have it out with them just as we did before.

Like photographs in the family album, the images of the dead populate the soul. The mourning process is the laboratory in which the images life has imposed upon the film of death are developed. Everything that has died and that we encounter as no longer there is the negative from which our inner life emerges. There is Elizabeth all in white, and me at twelve, and me again at twenty. Whole boxes of negatives that have never been printed, never been grieved. But now this immense loss, this loss in which I'm lost, holds me in the darkroom of the mourning process until all the lost souls come back to life in the emulsion of the mind.

REFERENCES

1. M.H. Abrams et al. (eds.), *The Norton Anthology of English Literature*, (3rd Edition), W. W. Norton, New York, 1962.
2. S. Freud, *The Interpretation of Dreams*, J. Strachey (trans.), Avon Books, New York, 1965.
3. S. Freud, Mourning and Melancholia, in *Collected Papers*, Vol. IV, J. Riviere (trans.) Hogarth Press and The Institute of Psycho-Analysis, London, 1924-1950.
4. J. Hillman, *Inter Views*, Harper & Row, New York, 1983.
5. S. Freud, *Letters of Sigmund Freud*, E. Freud (ed.), Basic Books, New York, 1960.
6. S. Freud, *Totem and Taboo*, in *The Basic Writings of Sigmund Freud*, A. A. Brill (trans.), Random House, New York, 1938.

10.20

CHAPTER 3

The Resurrection of the Dead: A Jungian Approach to the Mourning Process

> Psychic existence and above all the inner images . . .supply the material for all mythic speculations about a life in the hereafter, and I imagine that life as a continuation in the world of images. Thus the psyche might be that existence in which the hereafter or the land of the dead is located [1, pp. 319-320].
>
> C. G. Jung

THE REALITY OF THE PSYCHE

Different ontological assumptions, different assumptions about how reality is to be defined, wear their mourner's bands on different sleeves. Although Freud and Jung both referred in their writings to an order of reality which they called "psychic" or "psychical," each meant something quite different by that term. For Freud, psychic reality was a secondary reality, an epiphenomenon which is reducible in its every aspect to biology. Jung, on the other hand, viewed the psyche as an order of reality in its own right. Though he did not deny the existence or importance of physical reality, he also did not devalue the psyche by looking outside it to biology for substantiation. For Jung, Freud's translation of the psyche's images into bio-sexual terms was unnecessary, since images, just as they are, are already psyche. Indeed, from Jung's perspective, any psychology that grounds itself in an order of reality outside the psyche's own images has committed the category error which Whitehead called "misplaced concreteness." Jung's famous phrase—"image is psyche" [2, p. 50]—means that it is in images that the psyche manifests itself most concretely. The psyche, for Jung, is "an *ousia*," a "substance, essence" [3, p. 540]. Regardless of whether the opinions, ideas, fantasies or feelings among which we live, move and have our being are "true" or not when judged in accordance with the truth criteria of other sciences, they are still *entities* for Jung, "like animals and plants" [4, par. 742]. As Jung put it [5, pp. 359-361]:

> "Physical" is not the only criterion of truth: there are also *psychic* truths which can neither be explained nor proved nor contested in any physical way. If, for instance, a general belief existed that the river Rhine had at one time flowed backwards from its mouth to its source, then this belief would in itself be a fact even though such an assertion, physically understood, would be deemed utterly incredible. Beliefs of this kind are psychic facts which cannot be contested and need no proof
>
> Religious statements are of this type. They refer without exception to things that cannot be established as physical facts. . . . Taken as referring to anything physical, they make no sense whatsoever. . . . They would be mere miracles, which are sufficiently exposed to doubt as it is, and yet they could not demonstrate the reality of the spirit or meaning that underlies them.
>
> The fact that religious statements frequently conflict with the observed physical phenomenon proves that in contrast to physical perception the spirit is autonomous, and that psychic experience is to a certain extent independent of physical data. The psyche is an autonomous factor, and religious statements are psychic confessions which in the last resort are based on unconscious, i.e., on transcendental processes.

From a Jungian point of view, the concept of resurrection is a *mythopoeic idea*, not merely a theological assumption. Indeed, like all religious statements it is as well a *psychic* truth. Just as the psyche might tell of itself in terms of a belief that "the river Rhine had at one time flowed backwards from its mouth to its source," it may tell of itself in the metaphorical terms of resurrection as well. Though the literal validity of resurrection as a theological assumption cannot be demonstrated, as a truth of the soul, 'resurrection' possesses a psychic reality which neither requires nor could acquire further validation beyond its own imaginal self-display. While science and religion may divide and polarize over such problems as the resurrection of the literal, the resurrection of the flesh, analytical psychology, providing it confines itself to the imaginal psyche—the realm 'between' matter and spirit—can provide a phenomenological description of the metaphors and images which underpin the psyche's relationship with death. Regardless of whether we subscribe to theological notions regarding the immortality of the soul or not, we mourn as if we did. In even the most stalwart of atheists, images animate bereavement as if they too populated a beyond.

As death brings the physical categories into which the psyche has been incarnated to an end, resurrection dawns. Psyche is the "death" in life and the "life" in death. Long after the body is gone, soul carries on, even as Freud and Jung, sustained now entirely by images, carry on. The bereaved are not the only survivors who require our care.

THE AUTONOMY OF THE DEAD

The differing conceptions of psychic reality held by Freud and Jung are the basis of the different status they each grant to the images which continue the existence of lost objects in the mind. When Freud deals with the images of the dead it is entirely with reference to the psychodynamics of the bereaved survivor. The image of a loss, for Freud, is exclusively a function of the needs and wishes of the bereaved patient who is suffering that loss and who had the image. For example, in his paper, "Formulations Regarding Two Principles in Mental Functioning," a paper in which he discusses the process by means of which the imaginal psyche comes to be ordered by the reality-principle, Freud recounts the dream of "A man who had at one time looked after his father through a long and painful illness up to his death" [6, p. 20]:

> . . . in the months following his father's decease he had repeatedly dreamt as follows: *his father was again alive and he was talking to him as of old. But as he did so he felt it exceedingly painful that his father was nevertheless dead, only not aware of the fact.*

Commenting on the dream Freud argues that [6, pp. 20-21]:

> . . . no other way leads to the understanding of this seemingly senseless dream than the addition of 'as the dreamer wished', or 'as a result of his wish', after the words 'that his father was nevertheless dead'; and the further addition 'that he wished it' to the last words.

Freud analyzes the dream to be a self-reproach on the part of the dreamer. The dream is simply reminding the dreamer of the desires he recently experienced that his father might die (and so be released from suffering) and also of the more infantile death-wishes he harbored for his father as a result of his Oedipus-complex.

But if we examine the dream again, this time with Jung's conception of psychic reality in mind, another way of understanding it suggests itself—a way which gives more importance to the psychology of the image "father alive again" than to the psychodynamics of the dreamer. For Jung, the literal death of an object does not terminate its psychological life. Indeed, it is only after the corpse of a loved one has been buried that we directly experience the image through which that loved one has been an experience for us. This is not to say that we produce the image psychodynamically or that the dreamer in Freud's example is merely talking to his own projection. From Jung's point of view, we do not "produce" images or "have" dreams any more than we produce the objective world. The images of the psyche produce themselves autonomously and spontaneously and cannot be reduced to our psychodynamics without remainder. On the contrary, our psychodynamics, as Jung has written, are to be reduced to these figures [2, p. 247].

To object that Freud's patient's conversation with the dream image of his father cannot be proven to be a posthumous conversation with his once corporeal father misses the point. From Jung's point of view, it is equally dubious to assert that the patient ever conducted a direct conversation with his corporeal father when his corporeal father was alive. Since all experience is mediated by the psyche, that "only category of existence of which we have *immediate* knowledge" [5, p. 480], the important thing, for Jung, is to realize that the psyche's images are as real and as worth talking to after the cessation of their incarnational life as they were during it.

In Jungian analysis, Freud's patient would be invited to dialogue with his dead father, just as he had spoken with "father alive again" in his dream. No interpretations would be made. Interpretation, as Freud's analysis of the dream bears witness, would merely render its images a function of the same psychodynamics and projections which attenuated their relationship when the father was alive. Instead of connecting to "father alive again" who is "nevertheless dead," interpretation, in its denial of death, would attempt to resuscitate the old psychology. Instead of staying with the image and keeping pace with what "father alive again" is now doing, interpretation would leave it for the Oedipus-complex, the father-complex and the stormy visions of other phantoms. But, as Shelley tells us in his poem, *Adonais*, as he sticks with the image of Keats alive again [7, p. 1798]:

> Peace, peace! he is not dead, he doth not sleep—
> He hath awakened from the dream of life—
> 'Tis we, who lost in stormy vision, keep
> With phantoms an unprofitable strife. . . .

Psychologically speaking, when an object dies, the image which had animated it is no longer bounded by it. *It* does not die; rather, the literalism which bound it to life dies. "[A]waken[ing] from the dream of life" means that the image has awakened into its own ontology. Just as the Keats of *Adonais* is no longer sustained by a substance other than poetry, the father in Freud's patient's dream is no longer sustained by a substance other than images. Both imaginal figures, having ceased to be a function of the literalized metaphors with which they mixed in life, now float as categories, integrities of souls, angels. And now, perhaps for the first time, the patient, who had learned through psychoanalysis to view himself as the son of his father-complex, may recognize himself instead as the son of this subtle, psychological father, a father who he has yet to get to know.

An imaginal approach to the mourning process attends to the process through which the *images* proceed. Its purpose, as Jung wrote in his psychological commentary on *The Tibetan Book of the Dead*, "is to enlighten the dead on their journey through the regions of the *Bardo*" [5, p. 537]. While other writers, most notably Elizabeth Kubler-Ross, have stressed the importance of finishing "unfinished business", the imaginal psychologist stresses the importance of beginning the business with the images that has not yet begun. What precisely is "father alive again" saying? What is it exactly that he wants?

Unfinished business cannot be resolved by going back in time. Indeed, our business with the dead will always feel unfinished if we try to meet them in a past which they no longer inhabit. From the imaginal point of view the dead are not in history. On the contrary, it is history which is in the dead. Our lives are haunted not so much by what once *was* as by *how* what was is and shall be. As the dead speak to us in our dreams and fantasies, the past manifests itself in the present where it can enact itself in novel ways.

Sometimes, when a patient's mourning process has atrophied it is because the patient is sticking to a historicized version of the image rather than to the image itself. Instead of connecting to the autonomous image as it moves through the imagination, the stuck patient rigidly recollects a memory image.[1] The widow who has kept her deceased husband's things exactly as they were when he was alive has cut herself off from experiencing her dead husband as an animating presence in her on-going life. Unable to imagine and be informed by how her husband might act today, she makes a museum out of the circumstances in which his actions were embedded in the past. Time stands still. Fresh images cannot break through. The putrid smell of death—not his but her's—pervades the room.

Therapy can address the patient's failure to accept the change which the loss of a loved one has occasioned by interesting the patient in the changes which that loved one displays now that his or her image is no longer bound to life. Helping the patient to imagine the changes in circumstance which the dream figures are becoming accustomed may help her come to terms with her own change in circumstances as well. Perhaps, when the patient recognizes that her late husband can appear in dreams in a fashion radically discontinuous with his previous life, she, too, will be able to imagine a new life for herself, a life in which she and he need no longer be restricted to their old roles.

Although the imaginal approach to the mourning process is a nostalgic approach, the nostalgia which it promotes is not sentimental. The patient who sentimentally laments the subjective dimension of a loss must come to recognize, with Jung, that "the land of the dead observes icy silence, unperturbed by the grief of the bereaved" [1, p. 321]. Though the Kleenex box and the compassionate heart have long been the mainstays of bereavement counselling, the dead are moved by images, not by tears.

Sentimentalized grief is the corollary of that type of melancholia which Freud described, in which the patient "knows whom he has lost but not *what* it is he has lost in them . . ." [8, p. 155]. Contrary to this type of melancholia, the sentimental patient knows what has been lost but not who has been lost *apart from that*. Due, partly, to a narcissistic style of attachment, the sentimental mourner has never known the deceased except in terms of how that person fulfilled or failed to fulfill the mourner's needs. Just as he was unable to acknowledge that the

[1] In the chapter, "On Life after Death", in his autobiography, *Memories, Dreams, Reflections*, Jung emphasized that the images of the dead are independent of our personalized memories: "The inner images keep me from getting lost in personal retrospection" [1, p. 320].

loved one had an individual life of his own when living, the narcissistic sentimentalist cannot recognize the individuating aspects of that loved one's death either. Railing against his loss, he continues to rage against any display of independence in the object even when that act of independence is to enter the grave. "Why has she done this to me?" "If he really loved me he wouldn't have up and died!" The orbit of sympathy spins furiously around the little self. What the loss of the love object has meant to the narcissistically fixated mourner is infinitely clearer than what or rather who that loved object was and is apart from him.

Who were they really? What did their lives signify and what do they now want? Death, by releasing our loved ones from the claims we placed upon them, makes a decisive contribution to their individuation and our own. As we shift our attention from ourselves to them, the awareness begins to dawn that they have a destiny beyond our tears. The psyche, as Jung observed [9, pp. 410-411], does not anticipate the ending of bodily life as a final end. Individuation continues beyond the grave.

PSYCHE AND PHYSIS

But what does Jung mean by "image" and what relationship does an image have to the lost object? Is it not a contradiction to speak of the dead as autonomous images on the one hand and to derive them from lost objects on the other?

Images, for Jung, are not "psychical reflections of external objects" [10, p. 442]. A dream image such as "father alive again" is not simply an epiphenomenon, a trace of the physical father left behind in the sensory apparatus. The dead are not merely memories or after-images. In equating psyche with image Jung intended "a concept derived from poetic usage, namely, a figure of fancy or *fantasy-image*, which is related only indirectly to the perception of an external object" [10, p. 442]. The psyche's images, in other words, are not reducible to sensory impressions. They are not still photographs of the object's *physical reality*. They are the substantiality of the soul itself. Although "father alive again" is discontinuous with the patient's *perception* of his father *as an external object*, as a poetic image this figure substantiates and continues the existence which the father has always had *as an imaginal being*. As Coleridge stated, it is only when "objects [are] perceived as objects" that they are "rendered fixed and dead" [7, p. 1588]. Psychic images refer to the images which animate objects, not to the objects as they are defined by physical categories; not, that is, to the objects *as* objects. Viewed imaginatively, objects are as well living images, and it is these living images that the images which animate bereavement, the images of the dead, immortalize. "Poetically dwells man on this earth" [11, pp. 283-284], exclaims Heidegger from the Beyond. Freud's patient's father, even while alive, was more than a external object; he was also a poetic or imaginal object and it is as a poetic or imaginal object that he now lives on.

When Jung referred to the images of the imaginal psyche as "the dead" he did not see them as continuing the existence of lost *objects* in the mind in the pseudo-material/quasi-psychic sense of Freud. The dead, for Jung, are images through which the life of the imagination continues despite the fact that the physical category into which its figures had been incarnated has been lost.

The relationship between the dead and the lost objects which once incarnated them is like the relationship between the dream-ego and the waking-ego. Just as the dream-ego is similar to the waking-ego and at the same time independent of it, figures such as "father alive again" are both like and unlike the deceased love-object whose imaginal existence they continue. It is not merely that these dead figures or images are "as real as [the bereaved patient]—as a psychic entity—[is] real" [12, p. 529]. "Father alive again" is as real as his objective correlative, the patients actual father, as imaginal or psychic entity, was and is real.

Although Jung distinguished between subjective dreams, in which the dream-figures refer to parts of the dreamer, and objective dreams, in which the dream-figures refer to the actual outer persons whom they resemble, his notion of the unconscious as the realm of the dead belies this distinction. When we realize that an outer object possesses an imaginal physiognomy or aesthetic face, we no longer need to make a decision about whether to view its behavior in dreams as making a metaphorical statement on the subjective level or an analogical statement on the objective level. ". . . In the deepest sense we all dream not *out of ourselves* but out of what lies *between us and the other*" [3, p. 172]. All dreams are "objective dreams" if their objective correlatives are viewed imaginally. As dreamers we are sleep-walkers in the *anima mundi*. And it is the dead who try to awaken us to this imaginal reality.

When Jung wrote to a bereaved correspondent that "Sooner or later all the dead become who we also are" [3, p. 343], he was not saying the dead are "introjects" in the Freudian sense. For Jung, it is not simply that at death our loved ones become incorporated into us. We become incorporated into them. The dead present the imagination in its purest psychic form. It is not that we grant them a semblance of eternal life by holding them in our memories. We imagine by means of them in accordance with the way they structure the imagination with their images. We are created in their likeness. As Jung put it, "Perhaps—who knows?—these eternal images are what men mean by fate" [13, p. 109].

ELEGIAC MOURNING

Since the images which continue the imaginal life of the deceased are poetic images, mourning is a poetic process. Being images in the poetic sense, the dead are insusceptible to physical decay and "survive" like poetry itself, "in the valley of [their own] saying" [7, p. 2614]. As Auden put it in his famous elegy for Yeats, if it were not for the "mourning tongues" of the elegiac imagination, "the death of the poet," or for that matter of any love-object regarded poetically, would extend to his poems as well [7, p. 2614].

Of course, the sorrow and woe of the bereaved may initially be so excessive that the elegiac imagination is suppressed. As Jung writes, "death is a fearful piece of brutality . . . brutal not only as a physical event, but far more psychically: a human being is torn away from us, and what remains is the icy stillness of death" [1, p. 314]. After the death of a dear one has been certified in terms of the appropriate physical criteria it may seem that the imagination has been pronounced dead as well. Bereft of images, the young widow may sit frozen in her chair, vacantly staring into space. A loved one's death may at first be simply unthinkable. Who are we without them? How can we go on now that they are gone? What will we do now? Having ceased to imagine in terms of the loved one now that he or she is "gone", we cease to imagine ourselves as well.

An imaginal approach to the mourning process is not a denial of the personal significance of a loss. However, being on the side of the psyche's images, its support for the depressive passions of the bereaved reaches its limit at the point where "The words of a dead man/ Are modified in the guts of the living" (Auden) [7, p. 2615]. A shadow side of the mourning process is that the bereaved may console themselves by re-inventing the dead in a fashion which is more pleasing. Like Stalin, they may place their own words in the mouths of the dead rather than accept what the dead are in fact saying. "He really was a Christian, despite his atheistic views," "He didn't really mean half the things he said." More innocently, the bereaved may make an orthodoxy of their personal image of the deceased and take offense if others entertain images which deviate from their own in any way. Or again, they may become angry with the autonomous activity of the imagination itself if in their fantasies the dead appear to them in strange or disconcerting ways.

Confrontation can play an important part in the facilitation of the mourning process, particularly when the psyche of the bereaved has become identified with the emotions of bereavement. The purpose of the mourning process is to locate the *im*personal aspects of our personal losses, and to do this the bereaved must see through what Hillman has called "the delusion of personal ownership of emotion" [14, p. 48]. When Jung wrote to a bereaved correspondent that "the dissolution of our time-bound form in eternity brings no loss of meaning[;] Rather does the little finger know itself a member of the hand" [3, p. 343], he was not articulating an emotional truth—despite its obvious emotional appeal—but an imaginal one. Experienced limbically, emotions seem merely personal, regardless of the fact they are archetypal and collective, common to all mankind. Excessive catharsis ignores the dead and wrongs our grief. The emotions of the mourning process cannot be differentiated and individuated without reference to the particularity of the persons who have been lost. In Jung's view, the task of psychotherapy is to find the images in which "our" emotions are psychologically grounded and dialogue with them.[2] When we examine the dreams of a patient sequestered in grief we typically find that the imaginal life of the dead has been upstaged by his intense ownership of the associated emotions. But when we switch to the vantage point of the dreams and include the dead in our understanding of the process, we may be surprised by what *they* are feeling. "Why do you weep so?" the angel asks. "Why do you pretend I am dead?" "Why do you abandon me with your tears?" Is it we who feel abandoned by them or they who feel abandoned by us? It all depends on whether the mourning process is examined from the "outside" as a clinical problem or from the "inside" as a poetic or imaginal one.

In his essay, "Tradition and the Individual Talent," Eliot writes that "Poetry is not a turning loose of emotion, but an escape from

[2] Jung employed this method in his own self-analysis or "confrontation with the unconscious": "To the extent that I managed to translate the emotions into images—that is to say, to find the images which were concealed in the emotions—I was inwardly calmed and reassured. Had I left those images hidden in the emotions, I might have been torn to pieces by them" [1, p. 177].

emotion, . . . not the expression of personality, but an es personality" [7, p. 2559]. The same could be said of the process. Although the bereaved may at first be unable to make a distinction between the emotions they are experiencing and their own personalities, the work of mourning requires that they find within their grief the images which immortalize the dead. "Impressions and experiences which are important for the man may take no place in the poetry, and those which become important in the poetry may play quite a negligible part in the man, the personality" [7, p. 2558], writes Eliot. Mourning, as a poetic process, attempts to free the impersonal from the personal in emotions and experiences. Much of what we recall about the dead is inconsequential so far as the psyche is concerned. Though an obituary may speak of the dead in the prosaic terms of "time, place, circumstance, cause and effect" (Shelley), the aim of the elegiac mode is to individuate the dead from the arbitrary aspects of their simply given lives, or better, to show the soulful necessity which has organized these contingencies, the lines of character on the face of fate. Above all, in their mourning the bereaved must take care to imagine the self-sustaining essence of the dead.

Though death cancels the life of the physical body, the body of images which our loved ones made for themselves and lived from carries on. Mourning is a miracle of faith, a miracle of faith in the life of images. Though "we" write the elegy it is always written partly in suspense. The verses surprise us. As mourners we merely crew upon the "ship of death" which our departed dear ones made to contain their dying. Indeed, when the voyage is particularly difficult it is sometimes because our loved ones built their boats poorly.

Finding the image in which an emotion inheres is the crucial step to locating its impersonal significance. It is also the crucial step in the making of a poem of lasting value. By taking the emotions out of both the life-history of the bereaved and the life-history of the deceased, and locating them in their inherent poetry, the mourner converts them into what Eliot called "*significant* emotion." The emotions of a mourning process which have been raised to elegy are as impersonal as the emotions of art [7, p. 2559]. And the mourner, like the poet, "cannot reach this impersonality without surrendering himself wholly to the work to be done[, and this he is] not likely to know . . . unless he lives in what is not merely the present, but the present moment of the past, unless [, that is to say,] he is conscious, not of what is dead, but of what is already living" [7, pp. 2559-2560].

THE COMMUNITY OF THE DEAD

The dead, if properly imagined and mourned, are not alone, for the psyche is densely populated. It is not just that we bury our loved ones in the earth beside their next of kin; we find them resurrected in the imagination in a similar fashion. In dreams and fantasies the dead appear in the company of other deceased relatives, as if death was not so much the loss of a family member as the occasion of that family's reunion. Of course, in many cases the "family" to which the souls of the dead are gathered extends far beyond the biological family. Resurrection, after all, is not the eternalization of the Oedipus-complex. With his *apotheosis* at Colonus even Oedipus made it to the collective unconscious. When imagining the dead the bereaved must locate them among the souls with whom they are archetypally related and spiritually akin.

Death is the final cause of love, its apocalyptic limit, its ultimate fulfillment, what mystics have called the face of the beloved. Whomever we have made soul with in our lives, whether we knew them in the flesh or only in the spirit, become at death our family. Even when the soul-making process has been a stormy one, marked by betrayals and desertions, a love that mourns may create from its own wreck the thing it contemplates. As Shelley put it so succinctly in *Adonais*: "die,/If thou wouldst be with that which thou dost seek" [7, p. 1802].

"I frequently have a feeling that [the dead] are standing directly behind us waiting to hear what answer we will give to them, and what answer to destiny" [1, p. 308], wrote Jung in his autobiography. Psychology, for Jung, was an elegiac discipline, an attempt, "ever renewed, to give an answer to the question of the interplay between 'here' and 'hereafter'" [1, p. 299]. His audience, whom he referred to as the "Unanswered, Unresolved, and Unredeemed" [1, p. 191], were already in the afterworld, albeit an afterworld few of his contemporaries could still believe in. And besides these there were "the dead [who] came back from Jerusalem, where they found not what they sought" [1, p. 378], and the tragic figure of Freud, a figure who is still difficult to mourn since he identified his soul with the reality principle. And now Jung, too, is "directly behind us," along with Paracelsus, Corbin and his other "next of kin," "demand[ing] to attain in death that share of awareness which [he] failed to win in life" [1, p. 309]. What is it that he wonders about today? What is the riddle that he poses by appearing to us now?

When mourning is conceived of as a cultural activity, culture itself can facilitate the process. The dead, whom the mourning process has already resurrected, may help us from the Beyond to mourn our most recent losses. A departed dear one, after all, is not a meaning unto himself alone. Indeed, "his significance, his appreciation," as a poetic image, "is the appreciation," as Eliot said of the poet, "of his relation to the [other] dead poets and artists" [7, p. 2554]. In the same manner as a new work of art enters its artistic tradition, the dead enter the afterlife of the imaginal psyche. "You cannot value him alone," writes Eliot [5, p. 524]:

> . . . you must set him, for contrast and comparison, among the dead. I mean this as a principle of aesthetic, not merely historical criticism. The necessity that he shall conform, that he shall cohere, is not one-sided; what happens when a new work of art is created [and, I might add, when a lost love-object elegized] is something that happens simultaneously to all the other works of art that preceded it. The existing monuments form an ideal order among themselves, which is modified by the introduction of the new (the really new) work of art among them. The existing order is complete before the new work arrives; for order to persist after the supervention of novelty, the *whole* existing order must be, if ever so slightly, altered; and so the relations, proportions, values of each work of art toward the whole are readjusted; and this is conformity between the old and the new [7, p. 2554].

A MYTH OF THE DEAD

In his psychological commentary on *The Tibetan Book of the Dead*, Jung writes of the soulless rationalism of modern man and of how it has dislocated him from "an elementary need which forces itself upon even the most 'enlightened' individuals when faced with the death of relatives and friends" [5, p. 523]. Not only have we lost the belief which constitutes the rational basis of a cult of the Dead—the belief in the supra-temporality of the soul, "the psychological need of the living to do something for the departed" [5, p. 523] has been rationalized away as well.

> Apart, however, from the masses said for the soul in the Catholic Church, the provisions we make for the dead are rudimentary and on the lowest level . . . We behave as if we did not have this need, and because we cannot believe in a life after death we prefer

nothing about it. Simpler-minded people follow their own gs and, as in Italy, build themselves funeral monuments of me beauty. The Catholic masses for the soul are on a level considerably above this, because they are expressly intended for the psychic welfare of the deceased and are not a mere gratification of lachrymose sentiments.

To understand the mourning process as it is suffered today, we must understand that, in addition to the particular loved one who has been lost, the bereaved have lost touch with the collectivity of the dead. If, today, it is especially difficult to find access to the mourning process, it is because we have become disconnected from the larger tradition of mourning. It is not merely that we are more alone in the modern secular world than ever before; our dead are more alone as well. Though science has not triumphed over death, it has had the audacity to demythologize it. Even when it does concern itself with the mourning process, it limits its field of vision to the "lachrymose sentiments" of the bereaved. These it measures and validates while the dead rot. But how can the living let go of the dead if there is no one in the "hereafter" to receive them? And how can the bereaved reassure themselves that their loved ones are all right at a time in history when inner voices have become synonymous with a psychiatric diagnosis?

Death, from Jung's point of view, is too important *not* to be talked about. Although well aware of the impossibility—on epistemological grounds—of ever acquiring certain knowledge of the "hereafter" or the status of the soul after death, Jung stressed the importance of formulating a myth of death [1, p. 302]:

> A man should be able to say he has done his best to form a conception of life after death, or to create some image of it—even if he must confess failure. Not to have done so is a vital loss. For the question that is posed to him is the age-old heritage of humanity: an archetype, rich in secret life, which seeks to add itself to our own individual life in order to make it whole.

The question posed by death from time immemorial down to the present is not a scientistic question. Indeed, like a Zen koan, the question—what will the afterworld be like?—seems absurd to rationality which recognizes only physical categories of explication. But, for Jung, this subversion of our narrowing rationalism is just the point [1, p. 302]. Death is an integral part of life, and if we are going to inhabit our lives fully, we must "have a myth which encourages [us] to look deeper into this whole realm" [1, p. 304].

Mourning, from a Jungian point of view, is a process of mythologizing about a life after death. Although the decease of our loved ones may not be facilitated by the wisdom of an ancient guidebook such as the *Bardo Thodol*, the images which animate bereavement can be understood as a *post hoc* attempt on the part of the bereaved to write one for them. Today, we have little more than those "experiences which make us thoughtful" [1, p. 312], our dreams and fantasies, to instruct us. But if we entertain these "hints from the unconscious" [1, p. 301], and mythologize in terms of them, the dead themselves may help us to initiate them into an awareness of "the primacy of the psyche, . . . that . . . one thing which life does not make clear to us" [5, p. 513].

REFERENCES

1. C. G. Jung, *Memories, Dreams, Reflections*, A. Jaffe (ed.), R. & C. Winston (trans.), Random House, New York, 1961.
2. C. G. Jung, *Alchemical Studies, Collected Works*, Vol. 13, R. F. C. Hull (trans.), Princeton University Press, Princeton, 1967
3. C. G. Jung, *Letters, Volume One: 1906-1950,* R. F. C. Hull (trans.), Princeton University Press, Princeton, 1973.
4. C. G. Jung, *The Symbolic Life, Collected Works*, Vol. 18, R. F. C. Hull (trans.), Princeton University Press, Princeton, 1976.
5. C. G. Jung, *Psychology and Religion: West and East, Collected Works*, Vol. 11, R. F. C. Hull (trans.), Princeton University Press, Princeton, 1958.
6. S. Freud, Formulations Regarding the Two Principles in Mental Functioning, in *Collected Papers*, Vol. IV, J. Riviere (trans.), Hogarth Press and The Institute of Psycho-Analysis, London, 1950.
7. M. H. Abrams et al. (eds.) *The Norton Anthology of English Literature*, W. W. Norton, New York, 1975.
8. S. Freud, Mourning and Melancholia, in *Collected Papers*, Vol. IV, J. Riviere (trans.), Hogarth Press and The Institute of Psycho-Analysis, 1950.
9. C. G. Jung, *The Structure and Dynamics of the Psyche, Collected Works*, Vol. 8, R. F. C. Hull (trans.), Princeton University Press, Princeton, 1960.
10. C. G. Jung, *Psychological Types, Collected Works*, Vol. 6, R. F. C. Hull (trans.), Princeton University Press, Princeton, 1976.
11. M. Heidegger, Holderlin and the Essence of Poetry, in *Existence and Being*, Introduction and Analysis by W. Brock, Henry Regnery, Chicago, 1949.

12. C. G. Jung, *Mysterium Coniunctionis: An Inquiry into the Separation and Synthesis of Psychic Opposites in Alchemy, Collected Works*, Vol. 14, R. F. C. Hull (trans.), Princeton University Press, Princeton, 1963.
13. C. G. Jung, *Two Essays in Analytical Psychology, Collected Works*, Vol. 7, R. F. C. Hull (trans.), Princeton University Press, Princeton, 1966.
14. J. Hillman, *Archetypal Psychology: A Brief Account*, Spring Publications, Dallas, 1983.

CHAPTER 4

Love and Sacrifice

Yet each man kills the thing he loves,
By each let this be heard
Some do it with a bitter look,
Some with a flattering word,
The coward does it with a kiss,
The brave man with a sword! [cited in 1, p. 5]

Oscar Wilde

LOVE AND DEATH

That love which lingers after death, communicating in verses with the images of the dead, manifests as well *before* that parting, in the grievous recognition that a relationship must be sacrificed lest its love be brought to ruin. Though a love-tie may release the soul to an expanded sense of life, sooner or later it may also attenuate it. Suffocating in the mingled breath of an exhausted affection, reduced to their lowest and most common terms, the lovers may long to set each other free, despite the fact that this setting free may constitute the death of their relationship. "Since thou and I sigh one another's breath,/Whoe'er sighs most is cruelest, and hastes the other's death" [2, p. 602], writes John Donne. Regardless of the subsequent, or even simultaneous relationships which may seem to have occasioned the ending of an affectional bond, the *meaning* for which a relationship has been severed ultimately resides in the relationship itself. Even if the relationship has not defaulted on the virtues which Paul associated with idealized love (*Agapé*), the virtues of patience, kindness, hope, belief, endurance, modesty and non-possessiveness (1 Cor. 13:4-7), we may find that we can sustain the love which has been made in a relationship only in the mourning of it. As Cleopatra puts it, a moment before she attaches a poisonous serpent to her breast: "The stroke of death is as a Lover's pinch, it hurts and is desired" [3, p. 1210].

It is as if that elegiac eros which conquers time, that love which loves the dead beyond the grave, had somehow been encoded in love's passions all along. The way we love each other after parting, the way we love each other after death, is not only present in the relationship we live before a death or parting; it is present as well in the passions which compel a relationship toward its death or parting as if toward a final consummation. Love is inherently elegiac. Though it demands our lives and commands our loins, it is impossible to fully incarnate its desire or actualize its passions. "The psychical value of erotic needs is reduced as their satisfaction becomes easy" [4, p. 187], writes Freud. "Possession for the most part becomes smaller through possessing" [5, p. 52], Nietzsche adds by way of explanation.

If an orgasm, as in the Renaissance view, is a "petite mort," a little death, it is not merely because the sexual act has depleted the libido or reduced the tension of the drives as Freud has suggested. An orgasm is a "little death" because the lovers are still alive. The reduction of sexual tension through what psychoanalysis has called "object-love" is not the goal of romantic love. Death is. Only in its sacrifice is love made fully actual. Only in the setting aside of the relationship in which it has been lived is love fully articulated. As Donne expresses it in "The Canonization" [2, p. 591],

> We can die by it, if not live by love,
> And if unfit for tombs and hearse
> Our legend be, it will be fit for verse;
> And if no piece of chronicle we prove,
> We'll build in sonnets pretty rooms;
> As well a well-wrought urn becomes
> The greatest ashes, as half-acre tombs
> And by these hymns, all shall approve
> Us canonized for love.

"If you love something set it free. If it comes back to you its yours; if it doesn't it never was," reads the pastel poster on a teenager's bedroom wall.[1] Love fulfills itself, less through our possession of the (apparent) object of its desire, than in the sacrifice of our designs upon the object. The biological crescendo of physical union always falls short of the spiritual crescendo which angels enjoy. As Blake, referring to angelic love, put it in *Jerusalem*, "Embraces are Cominglings from the Head even to the Feet, And not a pompous High Priest entering by a Secret Place." The eros of angels is the eros of elegy, an eros in which lovers come together in the imaginal union of an imaginal love. Though life may breed a host of antinomies, antinomies which attract each other through their very opposition, it is in death that they finally marry. As Shelley put it "Die,/If thou wouldst be with that which thou dost seek" [2, p. 1802].

Eros is eternally idealistic. The moment *we* experience satisfaction or fulfillment love passes beyond *its* eschatology. As Oscar Wilde put it, "The only thing worse than not getting what you want is getting it." In order to dispel the "post-coital sadness" which is occasioned by having gotten what we want we must imagine a new love-object or erect a new ideal in terms of which the old object may be revalued. As Keats writes: "Let me not wander in a barren dream, But when I am consumed in the fire,/Give me new Phoenix wings to fly at my desire" [2, p. 1835].

A love that can forfeit the relationship in which it is enacted, a love which refuses to place the relationship itself above the destiny of the persons who have become embroiled in its passions, is a love congruent with the necessities of Eros. The power of love, as Jung rightly surmised, resides in the abnegation of the power principle [7, p. 53]. Though we may will that a relationship continue indefinitely, we may discover, contrary to our wishes, that we must sacrifice a union—either fully or in part—or lose our capacity to love. "I cannot bear what your loyalty is costing you," she tells him. "Leave me now, go!" "It's like I'm knocking my head against a brick wall," he laments. "No matter what I say she is resolved to leave." Even when parting is "sweet sorrow," as it was for Romeo and Juliet, it is because as Jung put it, " . . . only that which can destroy itself is truly alive" [8, pp. 73-74].

Despite the intensely personal feelings to which lovers find themselves subject, love, as antiquity has taught, has an impersonal aspect as well. Eros, in the Greek view, is a cosmogonic force. In Hesiod's

[1] An American T-shirt slogan puts the point in a more psychopathic manner: "If you love something set it free. If it doesn't come back to you hunt it down and kill it."

Theogony Eros (along with Ge, Tartarus, Erebus, and Night), is among the first descendants of the original Chaos.[2] As Aristophanes, underlining the primacy of Eros states, it was not until "... Eros, the desirable, burst forth like a swift whirlwind . . . [and] . . . mingled in broad Tartarus with Chaos. . . . . [that] the immortal race of the blessed gods came into being" [cited in 9, p. 25]. The archetypal patterns which underpin existence are themselves underpinned by love. Eros, as the principle of attraction and commingling, comes first. Indeed, like the color spectrum into which white light is refracted as it passes through a prism, the archetypes of the collective unconscious, the forms of cognition, and the gods of myth and religion are the spectral differentiations of that original and originating love. And so, if we are not immune to identification with the archetypal patterns which style our loving, it is, as the myths illustrate, because the gods themselves are not immune to Eros either. Cupid's arrows pierce the limbs of the immortals as easily as they pierce the limbs of man. Ichor mixes freely in our blood. As Holderlin writes [cited in 10, p. 414]: "... shamefully, A mighty force wrenches the heart from us, For the heavenly each demand sacrifice."

We are more often possessed by love than in possession of it. Like Jung, we ". . . falter before the task of finding the language which might adequately express the incalculable paradoxes of love" [6, p. 353]. And so *we* become love's language, our lives but the metaphors and tropes through which its words become flesh. But as we die to one another, we differentiate out the human from the divine. This does not mean that we love less. On the contrary, we love each other better when we realize that although as metaphors of love we have initiated each other into loving, we are not Love's objects.

Love is philosophical. Although it may reflect itself in a variety of persons, this reflective activity is part of a larger process which culminates finally in the intellection of the forms. As "Socrates" puts it in the *Symposium*, one who wishes to be initiated into the mysteries of love should at an early age begin to approach beautiful bodies, ". . . then he should take notice that the beauty of one body is akin to the beauty in another body." Noticing that the beauty of one body is akin to the beauty of another body he must begin to "pursue beauty in essence . . . and relax the intense passion for the

[2] Othello says with reference to his beloved Desdemona: "... and when I love thee not, Chaos is come again" (*Othello* III. iii).

one." Gradually, as he comes to realize that love inclines him not to the object as it is physically defined, but to an essence that is non-physical, "he must believe beauty in souls to be more precious than beauty in body." Again and again, the object of desire, must be seen through and sacrificed to a more embracing intuition, until finally the adept "may see . . . the beauty of different kinds of knowledge" [11, pp. 104-105].

Although "Socrates" does not refer explicitly to the Eros of the *Theogony*, his depiction, nevertheless, is consistent with Hesiod's. Love is a way to knowledge precisely because it is the primary ingredient or force in the creation of the universe in which we live and of the gods who are its ordering principles. The movements of our love—its waxing and waning, its attractions and revulsions—if rightly understood, disclose knowledge of the universe and knowledge of the gods.[3]

The Socratic/Platonic notion that Eros is a way to the forms is similar to Jung's idea of the psychoid nature of the archetypes. Indeed, all three thinkers may be describing the same thing in their own ways. Just as "Socrates" maintained that an adept will first be attracted to the physical objects of the sensible world and then, having noticed the formal characteristic which these objects have in common, to the super-sensible forms of the mind itself, Jung maintained that psychic life spans a continuum which merges on the one end with *physis* and on the other with the archetypes of the collective unconscious [13, pp. 215-216]:

> Just as the "psychic infra-red," the biological instinctual psyche, gradually passes over into the physiology of the organism and thus merges with its chemical and physical conditions, so the "psychic ultra-violet," the archetype, describes a field which exhibits none of the peculiarities of the physiological and yet, in the last analysis, can no longer be regarded as psychic.

At the infra-red end of Jung's continuum the Socratic lover falls in love in a very compulsive manner according to the dictates of instinct and the biological "patterns of behavior." At the ultra-violet end of Jung's continuum, however, the Socratic lover is able to imagine his desire and to hold his desire in the imagination. The images

[3] For a thorough discussion of the inhibiting role of revulsion in a self-limiting eros see a work by James Hillman [12, pp. 72-79].

and ideas which characterize this region of the continuum reflect the physiological processes of the other end and provide meaning. Here at the ultra-violet end of the psychic continuum, as at the end of the Platonic line of cognition, love is no longer blind. As Jung put it, the archetype is an "instinct's perception of itself" [13, p. 136], the "spiritual goal toward which the whole nature of man strives" [13, p. 212].

The impossibility of a relationship bears witness to the transcendental character of love. Although we may attempt to enhance a bond through the cultivation of virtue or the honing of communication skills, neither of these measures is enough to sustain the love which has been its portion. Indeed, the very idea that love is something that needs to be sustained through human effort ("working on the relationship") is an idea incongruent with love's cosmogonic force. Love, as the myths illustrate, is not a function of our relationships. On the contrary, our relationships are a function of love. Eros is self-sustaining. It comes and goes according to its own erotic logic and will not confine itself unchanged to the limits of any relationship forever. As Shelley writes [14, p. 140]:

> Narrow
> The heart that loves, the brain that contemplates,
> The life that wears, the spirit that creates
> One object, and one form, and builds thereby
> A sepulchre for its eternity.

As life moves through its changes and archetypal phases the love which underpins existence changes as well. We are attracted to life in different ways, enticed toward our individuation through new affiliations, while the old relationships hold fast. But fissures develop. We no longer want the same things. Love no longer requires us in the same manner. We discover that our union is now at odds with life and, therefore, at odds with the love that once initiated us into life. Holding fast to one another, regardless of a change in the archetypal background of our lives, wrongs our love. Although we are always reluctant to give up a love-object we must accept and mourn that the relationship is over, lest through identification we become its caricatures. As Antony, realizing—too late—that he must break from Cleopatra, declares, "These strong Egyptian fetters I must break or lose myself in dotage."

No matter how precious a relationship has been, if it cannot sacrifice itself to the purposes of that larger love-affair which love conducts with life, persistence in it results in a "gruesome twosome." Fidelity is a hollow virtue if it is applied to a relationship which has been pierced by a leaden arrow.[4] It is life and love that we need to keep faithfully together, whether by taking new partners or by loving the same one under a new star.

MURDER AND SACRIFICE

> *What is Living?*—Living—that is to continually eliminate from ourselves what is about to die; Living—that is to be cruel and inexorable towards all that becomes weak and old in ourselves, and not only in ourselves. Living—that means, therefore, to be without piety toward the dying, the wretched and the old? [5, p. 68]
>
> Nietzsche

Sacrifice is essentially a life-affirming action. It is an attempt to disidentify our lives and love from the attitudes and/or relationships in which they have become stagnant. Appreciating that change and death are an inherent part of life, we agree to let go of one style of loving *in order to affirm another*. The loss, of course, is real—else it would not be a sacrifice. But the new life which we affirm through the sacrifice is real as well.

By itself renunciation is not enough. For an event to be called a sacrifice, it must also restore a sense of sacredness to life. Somehow, the renunciation must make life richer. After a relationship or *an overly personal attitude toward a relationship* has been sacrificed, the ongoing life of the lovers must clearly show that it was indeed better to have loved and lost than never to have loved at all.[5]

By giving up the particular object of affection, the sacrificer commits it to the symbolic order where it continues to inform him as an image

[4] This is not to say that morality is not extremely important. As Adolf Guggenbuhl-Craig points out, when Eros is lacking morality, "that erstz Eros," can fill in for it. However, morality is misused if it is deployed as a defense against our love [15, pp. 84-88].

[5] Whether it is an attitude toward the partner which must be sacrificed or the relationship itself is a complex problem. The greater the discrepancy between the archetypal ground of the relationship and the archetypal phase of life, the more likely it is that the relationship itself will be sacrificed.

within his love. The way we value a love-object in the course of changing it or detaching from it determines the quality of our subsequent loving. Indeed, as the attachment theorists have suggested, we are only as capable of forming affectional bonds as we are capable of mourning broken ones. Cupid's wings are the angelic wings of elegiac mourning. From the cradle to the grave our love is cradled in the grave.

The love which has been actualized through its own renunciation persists in the psyche as the holy ideal in terms of which a new relationship—either with the same partner or a subsequent one—is conceived. Through sacrifice, a romantic object-choice is changed from the signified object in which love sought its fulfillment to a floating signifier or arrow of desire. Sacrificed love, in other words, becomes the psychic category in terms of which new trajectories of love are aimed and fired. This does not mean that the new lover is measured against the old—although this may frequently appear to be the case. Rather, new love objects are loved with reference to the values which have been affirmed through previous sacrifices. Being the better for having loved and lost, we can never fall victim to the shadows of love *through the same life redundancies*. Inasmuch as a renunciation has truly been a sacrifice—its loss imagined and new life affirmed in the process of detachment—our compulsion to repeat its specific erotic process will cease. The allure of the living and the halo of the dead are now one. We love one another only insofar as we have sacrificed Eros.

Murder differs from sacrifice in that it neither renounces nor consecrates. Contrary to sacrificial love, the romantic murderer kills in order to better possess the object. Othello is a classic example. Believing Desdemona to have been unfaithful to him, he takes her life as a means of keeping her true. Standing over her while she sleeps, Othello resolves to smother her in order to render the innocent countenance she wears in her sleep eternal: "Be thus when thou art dead, and I will kill thee, And love thee after . . ." [3, p. 1037], *Othello* V,ii,18-19. While the sacrificial lover renounces attitudes or relationships out of a recognition that they have become anomalous to life, the romantic murderer views life as the anomaly and puts it to the sword. Unable to manage loss, the amorous murderer construes his beloved to be unfaithful whenever she fails to act in accordance with his idealized image of her. At bottom, of course, the problem is an inability to mourn. Devastated by early losses, the narcissistic lover is unable to live with his Desdemona because he is unable to live without his idealization of her. Again and again, the changes which are an inevitable part of life threaten the lover's relationship ideal and arouse his jealousy. Even if there is no actual third party, the lover feels cuckolded by life itself whenever his beloved responds more faithfully to its realities than to his need for object-constancy and stasis. Any change that the lover is unable to mournfully embrace and work through afflicts his consciousness in the form of paranoid suspicions. For when a lover's eros is unable to "die and rise the same, and prove/Mysterious by this love" [2, p. 591] it is vulnerable to the insinuations of an Iago. Sexual indiscretion with a Cassio becomes the explanation of every vicissitude and letdown. By killing his Desdemona the Romantic murderer endeavors to take her out of the arms of life and restore her to the fidelity of the *Liebestod*. In death he attempts to secure the static, loss-free relationship which he could not secure in life.

Sometimes, when doing therapy with a couple who are locked in such a death-grip, it is useful to prescribe a sacrifice.[6] After the destructive behaviors have been identified, a contract can be made between the partners that they will leave the relationship should they again behave in the ways that have been identified as damaging. In agreeing to this format the couple implicitly agree to sacrifice and change something. Either they renounce the attitudes toward their relationship which underpin its destructiveness or they renounce each other as partners. Immediately, the focus of therapy, no matter which sacrifice is made, becomes the facilitation of a mourning process. The couple must be helped to mourn the losses which the contract heralds.

A subtler character than the romantic murderer, and one met more frequently, is the "Pale Criminal." The name "Pale Criminal" is a name Nietzsche gave to people who are equal to their deeds when they commit them, but later find that they cannot endure the images of their deeds [16, p. 65]. A lover, for instance, becomes a pale criminal whenever he attempts to justify his ending of a relationship by invoking pseudo-motives. After willfully subverting the style of a relationship or severing a bond altogether, he stands before his superego or "red judge" and invents a guilty motive for his actions. "I just wanted to try it with someone else." "I wanted to take revenge." "It was only sex." But as Nietzsche explains, the "madness" that is admitted is a pale, insipid version of the instrumental madness that came "*before* the deed," the robust madness which is, at bottom, the will to life. Sexual indiscre-

[6] This intervention, innovated by the strategic school of family therapy, must, of course, be used with great care. I believe that it is best to use it within the larger framework of mourning.

tions, acts of vengeance, and betrayals committed as if due to moral weakness, are pale versions of the erotic madness which incites us to court life and change. Eros is ruthlessly committed to life. It is a daimonic force that will not be domesticated. And yet, it is not Eros which is responsible for the weal and woe of our domestic lives. We are. We do more violence to each other by pleading guilty to love's lesser crimes than to its capital ones. Better to be convicted of the stormy passions of life and love than to use the necrophilic virtues of Love's guilty accomplice, the Pale Criminal, in order to reduce a life sentence. As Nietzsche writes [16, p. 65]:

> Your killing . . . should be a mercy and not a revenge. And since you kill, see to it that you yourselves justify life!
>
> It is not sufficient that you should be reconciled with him you kill. May your sorrow be love for the Superman: thus will you justify your continuing to live!

EROS AND PSYCHE

The breakdown of a relationship and the establishment of a new or renewed bond is the subject of Apuleius's tale, *Eros and Psyche*. According to Apuleius, Psyche, the mortal wife of Eros, has never seen her husband. Though she enjoys rapturous nights in his arms she has never beheld him with her eyes. Hearing this, Psyche's jealous and mean-spirited sisters suggest to her that Eros may be an evil monster. Rattled by their insinuations, Psyche resolves to discover whether this is in fact the case. Late that night, after Eros has fallen asleep, Psyche lights a lamp and brings it close to him. As the light falls across the sleeping daimon, Psyche is startled by what she sees. Her husband, far from being a monster, is actually a beautiful young god. The unexpected sight of his beauty gives Psyche such a start that the lamp becomes unsteady in her hand and hot oil spills from it onto the beautiful Eros, scalding his wing. Awakened by the burning oil, Eros immediately rebuffs Psyche for having looked at him. (Earlier she had made him a promise never to do so.) Leaving the relationship, the outraged Eros flies back to his mother Aphrodite's palace to lick his wounds and mend his scalded wing.

The present tense is surely the appropriate tense for a tale that enacts itself so ubiquitously in our lives. Again and again as lovers we find that our love is unable to bear the psychology of our relationships and vice versa. As in Apuleius's tale, the problem begins the moment that the light of psychological awareness brings the erotic factor to consciousness. Although Eros loves Psyche, Eros is not psychological. And, likewise, although Psyche reflects the compulsions of Eros, Psyche is not erotic. Little wonder that the two make such uneasy, yet passionate, bedfellows. While Eros, being Socratic, seeks connection with the archetypes or forms, Psyche reflects in images the *contingent relativity* of what Eros has actually connected with. The love problem is familiar enough: though the lovers can see each other all too clearly via the light of Psyche's lamp, having mistaken one another for love's object they are each unable to see the transpersonal dimension of their partner's yearning. Inasmuch as the archetypes, as Jung wrote, are impersonal and trans-psychic [7, pp. 98-99], love's spiritual impulse cannot be reduced to the least common terms of its agent's psychic equation. Love is always somehow greater than the sum of its parts, and this is the fatality with which it wounds us. When the light goes on in the bedroom, the starlight disappears with the result that Love loses its bearings and becomes embroiled in psychic complexities. Of course, the vicissitudes of human relationships do offer rich possibilities for making soul, but, ultimately, the reach of Eros always exceeds the grasp of soul-making. The cliche is true if its sentimentalism is seen through: again and again, Love does conquer all—even its own relational ground.

In his tribute to Eros, the "Socrates" of the *Symposium* neglects to mention the bitterness of those reflective moments in which lovers realize that the (apparent) object of their affections is not the "thing-in-itself," but rather an object within a class of similar objects. Although Eros is a way to the forms as the Platonic view suggests, the adept is hardly immune to loss. As Freud put it, ". . . man never willingly abandons a libido-position, not even when a substitute is beckoning to him" [17, p. 154]. The process through which Eros detaches itself from a love-object and falls in love again—with the same or another partner—on the next higher logical level is a complex one. Typically, there is a period of mourning. While in some cases the lover feels let down by the love-object, in other cases he finds that regardless of even a positive estimation of the object he doesn't like himself in the relationship. One wing or the other is scalded.

After Eros leaves her, Psyche despairs. Without Eros, without love to give meaning to her soul, Psyche wastes and suffers. At a particularly low point she attempts suicide by drowning, only to be spared by the river spirit and counselled by Pan. Later, after learning that Aphrodite is searching for her to exact revenge for the hurt Psyche caused her son, Psyche journeys to Aphrodite's palace and throws herself upon the mercy of the goddess. The rest of the tale concerns the arduous labors which Psyche completes at the behest of her cruel mother-in-law. First, Aphrodite assigns Psyche the task of separating a heap of mixed seeds—a seemingly impossible task. Stupefied by the immensity of the ordeal, Psyche sits forlorn beside the seeds. But just as Pan had appeared to her earlier in her hour of need, a colony of ants takes pity on her now and completes the task for her. Chagrinned by Psyche's success with the seeds, Aphrodite assigns her a second task, this time a dangerous one. Psyche is to collect fleece from the monstrous sheep of Helios. Again, Psyche despairs and goes to a cliff in order that she may hurl herself to her death. But a reed speaks to her and tells her that if she waits till the sheep fall asleep at noon, she can collect their fleece from the branches and twigs they have rubbed against. The third task is still more dangerous, and Psyche initially approaches it as an opportunity for suicide as well. From a dangerous mountaintop she must brave a deep abyss and draw water from the icy river that flows below. This time the help comes from Providence, the bird of Jove, who flies down to the water with a crystal cup which Aphrodite had provided and brings the water back to Psyche. The final task assigned Psyche is to descend into Hades and bring back a portion of Prosperine's beauty in a tiny casket. Again Psyche responds to the task with thoughts of suicide, this time endeavoring to throw herself off a tall tower. But, just as before, a voice persuades her to persevere with her task and tells her how it may be accomplished. Psyche goes to the underworld, finds Prosperine, and is given the cosmetic substance which Aphrodite had commissioned her to retrieve. This time, however, she does not follow the instructions to the letter. The helpful spirit had instructed her not to look into the casket which contained the portion of Prosperine's beauty. Overwhelmed by curiosity, even as she had earlier been overwhelmed by a curiosity to see Eros, Psyche opens the casket and peeks inside. Instead of the expected cosmetic Psyche discovers that the casket contains "a hellish and truly Stygian sleep" [18, p. 50], the sleep of death. Significantly, it is at this point, the point at which Psyche has fallen dead in her tracks, that Eros recovers from his wound and comes to her rescue. After wiping the sleep from her and replacing it in the casket, Eros pricks her with one of his loving arrows and awakens her to a new relationship with him.

Psyche's labors are the labors of a soul bereft of love. No matter what the task—separating seeds, collecting fleece, drawing water, descending to Orcus or Hades—without love they are impossible for the soul. And yet, in the tale at least, Fate is benevolent. Although she repeatedly finds herself on the brink of suicide, Psyche is always dissuaded at the last moment from taking her life by the appearance of helpful spirits who provide her with new imaginative possibilities. It is not that the helpful spirits have a special knowledge. It is the impossibility of each situation in and of itself which counsels or effects a change in Psyche. *Inasmuch as Psyche perseveres in the impossible work of mourning, she is re-made by its impossibilities* to the extent that she can again attract the love of Eros [12, pp. 92-107].

The suicidal ideas to which Psyche finds herself subject *are* her helpful spirits. Indeed, it is only when she is at the absolute end of herself, only when she is on the brink of death, that the fresh perspectives of a new life dawn. As Hillman has put it, "From the evidence which the psyche produces out of itself, the effect of the death experience is to bring home at a critical moment a radical transformation" [19, p. 76]. When Psyche peeks into the casket which contains Prosperine's cosmetic, she is radically transformed by the beauty of death.[7] Lying still in her "Stygian sleep," utterly devoid of life attachments, Psyche can once more reflect the idealism of Eros and the compulsions of love—at least until her sisters call again and the whole pattern repeats itself on yet another Platonic level.

TRANSFERENCE

> Many die too late and some die too early. Still the doctrine sounds strange: 'Die at the right time' [16, p. 97].
>
> Nietzsche

In psychotherapy the patient and therapist foster a relationship with one another which they both know is going to end. Like life itself, therapy is finite. Indeed, when compared with the patient's life it is exaggeratedly so. In the consulting room weeks are abbreviated into fifty-minute hours, decades into a few months or years.[8] Ironically, it is

[7] For a fuller treatment of the psychological significance of Psyche's descent to the underworld the reader is referred to the work of James Hillman [12, p. 102] and Marie-Louise Von Franz [20, p. 128-129].

[8] Lacan intensified the relationship between the terminal nature of the analytical relationship and death with his innovation of the brief session. In Lacanian analysis, the session can end at any moment. The session may last an hour or only a few minutes. The analysand must free-associate with death.

within the context of these strict time limitations that the patient discusses the manner in which time has run out in his other relationships. Of course, there is never enough time for this relationship either. The session ends before the patient has really had a chance to tell his story. But just this, the finitude of relationship, *is* his story. Loss is not merely something which the patient struggles with in life and discusses in therapy. It is an experience toward which the therapy itself is building. Therapy compounds the separation-anxiety which the patient experiences as life moves through its changes by constantly reminding him of its own impermanence. By condensing time psychotherapy ensures that the patient will suffer from the therapy in the same way that he suffers from life, and kindles an eros which can only be dealt with elegiacally. It is not simply that the therapeutic relationship is as marked for death as all the patient's other relationships. *The therapeutic relationship is a special relationship in that it has been deliberately created in order to be sacrificed.* While all relationships eventually fall victim to the "arrows and slings of outrageous fortune," in therapy an attempt is made to conduct a relationship which is conscious of its terminal nature.

Although we humans are supposed to differ from other animals in that we know we are going to die, as individuals we routinely repress this awareness in order to get on with our animal lives. As Freud observed, "Our own death is . . . unimaginable, and whenever we make the attempt to imagine it we can perceive that we really survive as spectators" [21, p. 15]. Of course, in writing these words Freud was referring to literal death. His words, however, take on an even deeper significance when applied to the *metaphorical deaths* which we each must go through in the course of our lives. Frequently, we find that we are unable to imagine the death of the particular style of life in which our souls have been incarnated. Despite the fact that fate has turned, paths have parted, and people have changed or died, we remain committed to our old identity. Like the old King in the fairy tale, we cling to power despite the redundancy of our essential attitudes. Where once we waged a lover's quarrel with the world, having "survived as spectators," we now wage a lover's quarrel with our symptoms. As one patient expressed it: "My soul has become identical with the impression which her life made upon it. I languish with her in depression."

The "Socrates" of Plato's *Phaedo* identifies the practice of philosophy with the practice of death: " . . . those who tackle philosophy aright are simply and solely practising dying, practising death" [11, p. 466]. The same could be said of psychotherapy. The patient comes into therapy in order to loosen his hold on life. A relationship or an attitude toward a relationship has become outmoded and needs to be surrendered. Although he may not at first be able to see it, the way he lives is getting in the way of his on-going life. The therapist's task is to facilitate the dying process which the patient has preferred to postpone. By helping him value an attitude or relationship enough to let it go when it has become redundant, by helping him to *imagine* his losses rather than identifying with them, the therapist attempts to facilitate a mourning process in the patient.

It is useful when doing therapy to think of symptoms as the death in the patient's life or the life in his death. The obsessive ideas, somatic complaints, repetitively destructive patterns of relationship, fears and phobias are all necrophilic defenses against loss. Like the depressed man quoted above, the patient's symptoms are his means of resuscitating outmoded forms of adaptation. The more anachronistic a patient is, the more at odds he is with the timely demands of his life, the more symptomatic he will appear to be. Just as Miss Haversham sits in her wedding dress amongst cobwebs and antiques, unable to absorb the fact that her wedding ended before it even began, we sit in our symptoms. The main problem with which therapy works is the problem of releasing the patient's desire from its confinement within a love which refuses to sacrifice itself, a love which refuses to die.

Redemption requires sacrifice. Again and again, desire must be released from the life which love has realized. In order for passion to sustain and guide, habit must be short-lived [5, p. 229]. As Nietzsche put it, "You must be ready to burn yourself in your own flame: how could you become new, if you had not first become ashes?" [16, p. 90].

The psychotherapeutic relationship is a sacrificial relationship. The relationship which is established between the patient and therapist is established for the specific purpose of being renounced. The therapist's acceptance of the patient, his attitude of "suspended disbelief," allows the patient to establish a rapport with the therapist which is simultaneously a rapport with his own imagination. As the patient shares dreams, free-associations and other intimate details about himself, the therapist becomes invested with the patient's fantasies until he becomes the psychic equivalent of the patient's symptoms. When the patient talks with the therapist he talks to all that has gone dead in his life as if it were not dead. In the sessions the dead obtain another kind of life. Not only do they appear in the dreams, they appear as well in the assumptions which the patient makes about the therapist. Mother and father, brothers and sisters, the patient at various ages which have been critical for his soul-making, teachers, lovers, and friends—all the persons with whom he once lived, moved and had his being and in whom his symptoms now live, move and have their being return. In the relationship with the therapist the patient loves and hates them all again, even as he loves and hates his symptoms. It is not that the patient and therapist are trying to figure out why the patient is the way he is through an analysis of the experiences with others which have shaped him. It is not the influence of the persons of our fate which therapy works to correct; rather, it is our literalistic mode of continuing to seek their influence and support *in a past which they no longer inhabit*. The patient's problem is with the present, not the past, for it is in the present that the past has gone dead. By welcoming the dead into its precincts, therapy provides the patient an opportunity to part from them in a manner which will preserve what is life-giving about their love. And by taking the patient's redundant attitudes seriously and even locating them amongst their next of kin through mythological amplifications, it allows the patient to die, if not at exactly the right time as Nietzsche would have it, at least for the right reasons.

Although a therapeutic relationship, as the altar upon which a number of attitudes, relationships, and symptoms have been sacrificed, may have taken on an ever increasing value for the patient and therapist, it too must "create beyond [it]self and thus [perish]" [16, pp. 90-91]. Just as any other relationship can degenerate into self-parody if persisted in unchanged despite the change which has transpired in life, therapy can degenerate into self-parody as well. The failure of a therapist to dissolve a therapeutic relationship when the process clearly shows that it is time for it to be dissolved is an act of professional misconduct no less reprehensible than sexual misconduct with the patient. In both cases, the therapist falls into the role of providing satisfaction for precisely the demands for love which he is supposed to be helping the patient to sacrifice. The therapist's job is to *sustain* desire so that it may return the patient to life, *not* to satisfy it himself with interminable therapy. Ideally, the patient should always feel himself let down by the therapist. Though he may have come to the therapist to get from him what he did not get in some other relationship, the reality is that the therapist is even less likely to provide these things. Only by ending their relationship can the patient and therapist bring it to its consummation. Only by releasing their desires from the orbit of the relationship in which it was aroused will they do right by them. Of course, the love which is affirmed in the parting will continue to inform the subsequent love of both the therapist and his now ex-patient. In a passage titled "Stellar Friendship," Nietzsche beautifully describes how the eros of those who have parted in love sustains them on their way and in some larger, almost cosmic sense contains and joins them.

> We were friends, and have become strangers to each other. But this is as it ought to be, and we do not want either to conceal or obscure this fact, as if we had to be ashamed of it. We are two ships, each of which has its goal and its course; we may, to be sure, cross one another in our paths, and celebrate a feast together as we did before,—and then the gallant ships lay quietly in one harbour and in one sunshine, so that it might have been thought they were already at their goal, and that they had had one goal. But then the almighty strength of our tasks forced us apart once more into different seas and into different zones, and perhaps we shall never see one another again,—or perhaps we may see one another, but not know one another again; the different seas and suns have altered us! That we had to become strangers to one another is the law to which we are *subject*: just by that shall we become more sacred to one another! Just by that shall the thought of our former friendship become holier! There is probably some immense, invisible curve and stellar orbit in which our courses and goals, so widely different, may be *comprehended* as small stages of the way,—let us raise ourselves to this thought! But our life is too short, and our power of vision too limited for us to be more than friends in the sense of that sublime possibility.—And so we will *believe* in our stellar friendship, though we should have to be terrestrial enemies to one another [5, pp. 216-217].

SACRIFICE AND THE GODS

But what is this "immense, invisible curve and stellar orbit in which our courses and goals, so widely different, may be *comprehended* as small stages of the way . . . "? What is it that unites us in our resolve to be divided? What is it that compels the sacrifice of an attitude or relationship?[9]

In Jung's view there are two principal backgrounds to sacrifice, adaptation to collective moral standards being the more obvious. Fre-

[9] For Nietzsche, of course, it is the will to power and the making of the *ubermensch*—the new as opposed to historical man—which compels and orients our sacrifice. It could be argued that the *ubermensch* and will to power were, for Nietzsche, symbols of what Jung called the Self.

quently we renounce a personal claim because it is at odds with the moral code of our society. When we make a sacrifice against this background the individuating aspects of our actions are obscured. Jung identifies this kind of sacrifice with the renunciations made at the behest of the super-ego of Freudian theory.

The second background to sacrifice is more individual. Here, personal claims are renounced because we "feel impelled to do so for painful inner reasons which are not altogether clear to [us]" [22, p. 260]. As Jung elaborates [22, p. 260]:

> These [inner] reasons give me no particular moral satisfaction; on the contrary, I even feel some resistance to them. But I must yield to the power which suppresses my egoistic claim.

For Jung, the power which suppresses an egoistic claim, the power to which we make sacrifice, is the archetype of the Self. Although the Self may correspond to the super-ego at times, it is not identical with it.[10] Indeed, we experience the Self most directly when its dictates conflict with the dictates of our other loyalties. In situations such as this, situations of excruciating conflict, the whole man is challenged. It is not simply that we need to make a sacrifice to avoid society's censure. When the Self is demanding a sacrifice it means that we must overcome something in ourselves in order more fully to be ourselves. Here collective morality, though still important, is of little use, since our conscience is troubled with the problem of becoming *individually* who we are.

The archetype of the Self, as defined by Jung, is the archetype which corresponds with the totality of the psyche, both conscious and unconscious. In the relationship of the ego-personality to this one archetype resides our relationship to the totality of archetypal factors which underpin existence. The Self "knows" us better than we know ourselves by "knowing" the archetypal factors which will demand recognition in our lives. There is an awareness in us, an awareness "which suppresses [our] egoistic claim[s]" in a manner which is congruent with a knowledge—Jung called it "absolute knowledge"—of what is "outside" us. Historical factors, current events, the tick of the biological clock, family processes, global tensions, changes in *Zeitgeist*, death: our

[10]For Jung the Self, despite is authoritative quality, is actually amoral and it is up to the ego to wrestle with the moral and ethical problems which this archetype of wholeness presents.

soul-making with one another cannot ignore these factors. Relationships with friends, lovers, wives, children, teachers, mentors, priests, doctors, therapists, animals, insects, plants, minerals and artifacts etc., must be congruent with the impersonal factors which underpin their larger sense of destiny and our own. All relationships are "stellar friendships." Again and again our attitudes and relationships must be sacrificed to the Self. As Jung writes [6, p. 325]:

> The decisive question for man is: Is he related to something infinite or not? Only if we know that the thing which truly matters is the infinite can we avoid fixing our interest upon futilities, and upon all kinds of goals which are not of real importance. . . . In the final analysis, we count for something only because of the essential we embody, and if we do not embody that, life is wasted. *In our relationships to other men, too, the crucial question is whether an element of boundlessness is expressed in the relationship* (my italics).

Like Nietzsche's "immense, invisible curve and stellar orbit. . . , " the Self, for Jung, "is a circle whose center is everywhere and whose circumference is nowhere." Like "God" it is centered in us in a manner congruent with how "God" is in all things. As Lord of the Dance, it presides over the movements of our love, eroticizing the ego, whether in attraction or revulsion, in accordance with its wider sense of life and meaning.

It is important to realize that while Jung defined the Self as the "empirical God-image in man," the concept is an inference from his own and his patient's experiences with *specific* god-images. Although comparisons with the God-images of monotheistic religions may convey some aspects of the Self-archetype, individuation, even if defined as the road to the Self, is a process of serial monotheism within a polytheistic context. The Self's monotheism is actually perspectival. Indeed, from the psychological point of view, it is not that the Self requires that we worship no other gods before it; rather, it is that we must not worship any god to the exclusion of the totality of gods. The Self is the polytheistic complexity of life which underpins the short-term monotheism of our actual being. The power which suppresses our ego's piety, the power which Jung called the Self, is always a function of the monotheistic one-sidedness of the ego. It is not just that the other gods want their due. The god which we have incarnated in a specific relationship may want free of the limitations of that relationship.

When our relationships become like organized religions the god in whose name we have been brought together sickens and dies. In order to continue to serve the god we may then have to dissolve the relationship's organization. Often, it is only at this point, the point at which the Self drives us to heresy, that we even realize that we have been related to one another through the religious function in the first place. Jesus' statement—"When two or three are gathered together in my name I will be there" (Matt. 18:20)—is true of the other gods as well. In unconscious relationships, however, we may only find out which god "has loved us into loving" when the relationship is breaking down.

NAMING THE GOD

> Could the longing for a god be a *passion* welling up from our darkest, instinctual nature, a passion unswayed by any outside influences, deeper and stronger perhaps than the love for a human person? [7, p. 133]
>
> C. G. Jung

In his book, *Two Essays on Analytical Psychology*, Jung tells the story of a woman patient who developed a transference to him which proved impossible to resolve through appeal to the woman's common sense and rational judgment. Regardless of the fact that she clearly knew that Jung was not her father and that she must sacrifice her daughter-like dependence on him, the projection stuck fast. This obstinacy fascinated Jung and he wondered what its purpose might be [7, p. 133].

> That it must have some purposive meaning I was convinced, for there is no truly living thing that does not have a final meaning, that can in other words be explained as a mere left-over from antecedent facts.

In order to find out what his patient's unconscious was trying to achieve through the transference relationship Jung decided not to analyze her fantasies or treat her projections, but rather, to allow the young woman to freely elaborate them in the faith that the transference would achieve its own resolution in its own way.

Jung reports that the patient's transference fantasies, freed from the encumbrance of reductive interpretations, became more and more fantastic. Although the dreams mostly referred to her relationship with Jung, the "Jung" they connected her to "seldom appeared in his natural shape." Indeed, sometimes he appeared as a being of supernatural proportions or as a very elderly man or then again as her father. In one dream the patient dreamt that she was a tiny child in the arms of its father who was a giant. The giant stood in a wheat field. As the wind swept over the field the giant swayed back and forth, rocking the child [7, p. 130]. Commenting on this dream, Jung suggests that the patient's subconscious, by endowing him with superhuman qualities, was attempting to objectivate the image of a specific deity, an "archaic . . . nature-daemon, something like Wotan" [7, p. 135].[11]

It is ironic that the impossible demands which the patient made in the transference were resolved by becoming even more impossible. While Jung found that no appeals to the young woman's common sense were able to curtail her daughter-like dependence upon him, he could, or rather her unconscious could, resolve this dependence without recourse to common sense by connecting her to the deity which, because of her agnostic attitude, she projected onto him. It is not simply that it was easier for Jung to hand back the projection that he was a god than to hand back the projection that he was a father. The young woman's unconscious, in Jung's view, "was trying to *create* a god out of the person of the doctor, as it were to free a vision of God from the veils of the personal . . . " [7, p. 133]. Although Jung could not be what the patient wanted him to be, although he could be neither her father nor her god, the deity that was animating the transference could be. Recognition of the religious content of the transference, in Jung's view, freed the patient from her dependence on the personal tie to the doctor. Presumably the young woman's daughter-like dependence could now give way to an attitude of religious dependence, not on Jung, but on that "transpersonal control-point" [7, p. 134] which Jung called the Self. Rocked in the arms of the individuation process, blown to and fro by the breath of the god, the young woman no longer needed the transference because her projections had connected her to their archetypal goals.

Jung's case is reminiscent of several stanzas from Tennyson's elegy "In Memoriam A. H. H." [24, p. 64]:

[11]Jung has written elsewhere that ". . . the Christian Weltanschauung, when reflected in the ocean of the (Germanic) Unconscious, logically takes on the features of Wotan" [23, p. 246].

As sometimes in a dead man's face,
To those that watch it more and more
A likeness, hardly seen before,
Comes out—to some one of his race;

So, dearest, now thy brows are cold,
I see thee what thou art, and know
Thy likeness to the wise below,
Thy kindred with the great of old.

But there is more than I can see,
And what I see I leave unsaid,
Nor speak it, knowing Death has made
His darkness beautiful with thee.

Just as Jung's patient likened him to a being of supernatural proportions, a nature daemon, and a god, the grieving Tennyson sees in the death-mask of his late friend a "likeness to the wise below." In both cases an archetypal factor appears which makes the renunciation of the personal tie possible. The grieving poet and the dependent patient may now sacrifice their personalistic tie to the love-objects with which they have become identified because there is something eternal to sacrifice them to. Call them the platonic forms of the relationships in which the soul was made. Call them ancestors, archetypes, gods. By letting go our terrestrial connection with them we consummate a stellar one. No longer are they so much the persons whom we love as they are the persons by means of whom we love. Look up to the heavens: there they are, watching over us, the fixed stars of our fate. Listen to your heart: there they are, counselling us with the wisdom of our self-overcoming.

REFERENCES

1. J. Bowlby, *The Making and Breaking of Affectional Bonds*, Tavistock Publications, London, 1979.
2. M. H. Abrams et al. (eds.), *The Norton Anthology of English Literature* (3rd Edition), W. W. Norton, New York, 1975.
3. W. Shakespeare, *William Shakespeare: The Complete Works*, A. Harbage (ed.), Penguin, New York, 1969.
4. S. Freud, On the Universal Tendency to Debasement in the Sphere of Love (1912), in *Standard Edition of the Complete Psychological Works of Sigmund Freud*, Vol. XI, J. Strachey (trans.), Hogarth Press and The Institute of Psycho-Analysis, London, 1961.

5. F. Nietzsche, *The Joyful Wisdom*, T. Common (trans.), Frederick Ungar, New York, 1960.
6. C. G. Jung, *Memories, Dreams, Reflections*, A. Jaffe (ed.), R. & C. Winston (trans.), Random House, New York, 1961.
7. C. G. Jung, *Two Essays in Analytical Psychology, Collected Works*, Vol. 7, R. F. C. Hull (trans.), Princeton University Press, Princeton, 1966.
8. C. J. Jung, *Psychology and Alchemy, Collected Works*, Vol. 12, R. F. C. Hull (trans.), Princeton University Press, Princeton, 1968.
9. M. Morford and R. Lenardon, *Classical Mythology*, (2nd Edition), Longman, New York, 1971.
10. C. G. Jung, *Symbols of Transformation, Collected Works*, Vol. 5, R. F. C. Hull (trans.), Princeton University Press, Princeton, 1967.
11. Plato, *Great Dialogues of Plato*, W. H. D. Rouse (trans.), The New American Library, New York, 1956.
12. J. Hillman, *The Myth of Analysis*, Harper & Row, New York, 1972.
13. C. G. Jung, *The Structure and Dynamics of the Psyche, Collected Works*, Vol. 8, R. F. C. Hull (trans.), Princeton University Press, Princeton, 1960.
14. P. B. Shelley, *The Complete Poetical Works of Percy Bysshe Shelley*, T. Hutchinson (ed.), Oxford University Press, London, 1914.
15. A. Guggenbuhl-Craig, *Eros on Crutches*, Spring Publications, Irving, 1980.
16. F. Nietzsche, *Thus Spoke Zarathustra*, R. Hollingdale (trans.), Penguin Books, Harmondsworth, 1961.
17. S. Freud, Mourning and Melancholia, in *Collected Papers*, Vol. IV, J. Riviere (trans.), Hogarth Press and The Institute of Psycho-Analysis, 1950.
18. L. Apuleius, *Amor and Psyche*, H. E. Butler (trans.), in E. Neumann, *Amor and Psyche: The Psychic Development of the Feminine*, R. Manheim (trans.), Princeton University Press, New York, 1956.
19. J. Hillman, *Suicide and the Soul*, Hodder and Stoughton, London, 1964.
20. M-L. Von Franz, *Projection and Re-Collection in Jungian Psychology*, W. Kennedy (trans.), Open Court, La Salle, 1980.
21. S. Freud, *Civilization, War and Death*, J. Rickman (ed.), Hogarth Press and The Institute of Psycho-Analysis, London, 1939.
22. C. G. Jung, *Psychology and Religion: West and East, Collected Works*, Vol. 11, R. F. C. Hull (trans.), Princeton University Press, Princeton, 1958.
23. C. G. Jung, *The Archetypes of the Collective Unconscious, Collected Works*, Vol. 9i, R. F. C. Hull (trans.), Princeton University Press, Princeton, 1968.
24. A. Tennyson, In Memoriam A. H. H., in *Victorian Poetry and Poetics* (2nd Edition), W. Houghton and G. R. Strange (eds.), Houghton Mifflin, Boston, 1968.

CHAPTER 5

BEREAVEMENT GUILT

In this last of meeting places
We grope together
And avoid speech
Gathered on this beach of the tumid river [1, p. 91]

T. S. Eliot

REGRET AND RESURRECTION

Intimately connected with the experience of loss is the feeling of guilt. When we renounce a relationship or grieve for a loved one who has died, we may reproach ourselves out of a sense of deep regret. "Why didn't I love him as well when he was living as I love him now that he is dead?" "Why didn't I tell her how I felt when I still had the chance?" "What right have I to live and love again now that he is gone?" Even when our lost loved ones did little to endear themselves to us we may find ourselves subject to the same sentiments. The same miserable creature who was despised by friends and family for his ruthless disregard of their needs and feelings may be celebrated after death as a principled man of uncompromising integrity. Likewise, the inconspicuous little woman who minded her own business and never bothered anyone may have her worth appreciated only after she is gone. Somehow, death transfigures our loved ones into images which compel our respect and before which we at first may feel unworthy. In a sense we are all born posthumously.

Of course, to outsiders who do not share the mourner's sense of loss these feelings may seem to be nothing more than defenses against the hostilities once harbored toward the deceased.[1] The psychoanalyst would consider these sentiments to be reaction formations grounded in denial. Appreciated from the inside, however, it is quite evident that something deeper is going on. The bereaved are not white-washing their old relationships with sentimentality; they are beholding the dead in the whitened bodies of their imaginal life. Now that our loved ones are dead their existence no longer upstages our recognition of their essence. We relate to them spiritually now, through the imagination, as integrities of soul. And the guilt we now feel may be dealt with spiritually as well—not by the expiation of past sin, but by at-one-ment with the ghosts which our guilt would connect us with.

THE CATEGORICAL IMPERATIVE

Kant's Categorical Imperative, "the supreme, absolute moral law of rational, self-determining beings" [2, p. 47], defines the essence of moral conduct as follows: "Act so that you treat humanity, whether in your own person or in that of another, always as an end and never as a means only" [3, p. 47].

Regardless of whether we have ever read Kant or not, there is something Kantian about our grief. When our loved ones die, we experience regret for having acted to use them as extensions of ourselves rather than as beings in their own right, ends in themselves. The guilt which loss occasions is based upon our transgression of the Categorical Imperative. The regrets of the bereaved are a function of the discrepancy between how they experienced their loved ones before their deaths and after. Although the various psychoanalytic accounts of guilt may contribute to our understanding of the neurotic distortions of the mourning process, it is important to recognize that variety of guilt which is metaphysical in the sense of Kant's *Metaphysic of Morals*, and thus, a legitimate part of the mourning process.

The guilt which accompanies the loss of another human being is never simply a function of super-ego condemnation. Nor is it merely the result of having turned upon ourselves the anger we feel toward the deceased for abandoning us. These theories of guilt are etiological. They understand guilt in terms of the vicissitudes of the survivor's life

[1] Freud advanced this account of the relationship between loss and guilt, interpreting dreams in which the deceased appear alive again as the dreamer's wishful evasions of the guilt occasioned by his previous death-wishes (see Chapter 3).

process. But the guilt of bereavement is a function of the images which animate bereavement, the images of the dead. The mourning process consists of a confrontation with death, an agonizing encounter with the meaning of specific beings at their physical end. The associated sense of guilt is eschatological. In bereavement we experience ourselves as the guilty accomplices at our loved one's Last Judgement, partners in the moral crime of mutual "usury." This eschatological vision of our loved ones shocks us out of our etiological stance into a more teleological view. The "essence" of our loved ones (rather than the "superego") disturbs our conscience. We are plagued by questions of meaning and purpose. What has our love meant to their death? What does their death now mean to our love? "As with the force of waters," the mind undergoes baptism and turns toward a new way of life (repentance in the Greek sense: *Metanoia*), a life informed by an eschatological encounter with our loved ones.

The guilt specific to a loss is as imaginal as the mourning process itself and derives its proportions from the images of the dead. Although we may have used our loved ones in a manner incongruent with their natures, confused their ends with our own (projection), and discounted their worth while they were alive, after death it is much harder to do so. In the afterlife of the imaginal psyche, the "Kingdom of Ends" (Kant), they stand for themselves. They are not available for our "use." We can no longer engage them in the world of means.[2] But now, perhaps for the first time, we can ask them what *they* want and realize what they mean. They return to us in dreams, appear to us in visions, talk to us from the edges of awareness. Ironically, it is only by passing away that they really fully get here.

THE SHOOTIST

The distinction between treating people as a means to some ulterior purpose and treating them in a manner congruent with their essence, congruent with their ends, is the theme of a John Wayne film titled, "The Shootist." Wayne is a famous aging gunfighter dying of cancer. He seeks out a boarding house in which to live out his last weeks in peaceful anonymity. However, word of his identity leaks out and one after another people come to see what they can get out of him. A

[2] Unfortunately, this is not always true. The dead are frequently used by the living as scapegoats for blame and as sources for self-glorification.

journalist wants to write an exploitative novel about him that will basically distort who he actually is. An old lover, who at first appears to love him and to want to nurse him through his illness, actually turns out to be in cahoots with the journalist who has promised to share with her the rights of the gunfighter's story. Various gunmen attempt to gain the glory and renown of killing Wayne in a shoot-out. Even the undertaker plans to turn the funeral into a side show so that he can charge admission to anyone wishing to view the dead man's body. But by the end of the film, Wayne has differentiated himself from the projections and designs of the other characters. We see that he is a man of great integrity and mark in him the passing of the Old West.

MR. HALPERN AND MR. JOHNSON

Another film that illustrates the difference between relating to people as a means and relating to them as ends in themselves is "Mr. Halpern and Mr. Johnson," starring Lawrence Olivier and Jackie Gleason. The bereaved Olivier meets the disenfranchised mourner, Gleason, at his wife's funeral. Although Gleason is unknown to him, it turns out that he was a friend of Olivier's wife. Olivier is interested to learn from Gleason how he came to know his late wife. He looks forward to meeting this new acquaintance and sharing stories that will take the edge off the long loneliness of his grief. When they meet for tea, however, Olivier is taken aback to learn that Gleason had been meeting his wife one afternoon each year for the past forty years. As they continue to talk, the peevish Olivier feels threatened by the dignified Gleason and accuses him of having had an affair with his wife. Gleason assures him that it was strictly platonic, but does rub Olivier's nose in his own hypocrisy. Olivier had apparently himself been a womanizer. As the story unfolds, the husband, who had related to his wife rather exploitatively, using her as a means to his own selfish ends, learns things about his wife he had never known. Gleason acquaints him with a side of her he had lacked the sensitivity to recognize. He reveals to the bereaved husband something of his wife's essence. There is guilt over the failure of recognition, but also healing of that guilt since the recognition, in this last of meeting places, is now happening. Though it is only two men at the table, the audience becomes increasingly aware of the presence of the late wife. As the two men imagine her more and more accurately, her spirit floats free.

(Special effects are not necessary to convey this.) Thus we see in each of these films that what begins as exploitation ends as mourning.

KANT AND THE SPIRIT WORLD

The link we are suggesting between the Categorical Imperative's emphasis on "ends" and the images which animate bereavement, the images or spirits of the dead, finds support in Kant's own thought. In his *Lectures on Metaphysics*, Kant presents the reasoning behind his belief in the immortality of the soul and in the existence of an "other world" which we inhabit spiritually [cited in 14, pp. 176-177]:

> The consciousness of the ego proves that life is not located in the body, but in a special principle differing from the body; that as a consequence this principle can continue to exist without body, and that its life is not thereby diminished but augmented. *This is the sole proof that can be given a priori*, and one drawn from the knowledge and nature of the soul comprehended a priori by us.

If we insert this idea into Kant's Categorical Imperative, the meaning of the Imperative, far from being changed, is more fully articulated. Since the soul is immortal, mortality cannot be confined to the situationalist ethics of the bodily perspective. Our essential nature is wronged if we fail to relate to one another in a manner congruent with the angels which we also are. Where the Imperative speaks of "end," read "essence," "image," "angel." The figures of our dreams and fantasies, the spirits which appear to us in vision, and the ghosts which haunt our grief are the presiding persons[3] of Kant's Categorical Imperative. Their appearance *as categories of the imagination* compensates our usual relationships with them. In our incarnational life we more often live by what Kant called the "hypothetical imperative" than by the Categorical. If we want to do so-and-so we need only do such-and-such. The people with whom we live, move, and have are being are merely a function of our designs upon them—more hypothetical than

[3] I say "presiding persons" and not "personifications" because these persons are prior to the Categorical Imperative. Without their souls the Categorical Imperative is merely a philosophical abstraction. The Categorical Imperative resides in their laughter and their tears, in the way they see things and the things they say. Like Corbin's active intelligences [5], these angels of revelation come first.

necessary. No wonder they return as pangs of conscience, impressing us in the wee small hours with a sense of their intrinsic value. We are haunted by them as "ends" to the extent that we failed to recognize the perspectives they embodied when they were alive. Freud was right, at least if we read him with Kant in mind: the dreamer does bear responsibility for what he dreams.[4] The manner and degree to which the dead are now present in their absence reflects back to us the manner and degree to which we were once oblivious of them in their presence. As Eliot put it in his poem "The Hollow Men," how will "those who have crossed/With direct eyes, to death's other Kingdom/Remember us. . . . " Will they remember us as "the hollow men/The stuffed men?" [1, p. 91].

Although Kant writes about an "other world," it is important to understand that he does not consider this "other world" to be different from this world in any substantive sense. The "other world" is this world viewed differently—" . . . as an end, never simply as a means" [cited in 4, p. 177]:

> Since the soul has through the body a sensuous view of the corporeal world, when freed from the sensuous view of the body it will have a spiritual view, and this is the other world. In going to the other world one does not enter a community of other things, as it were on another planet, one stays in this world but has a spiritual view of everything.

The profane world, the world of means, reveals itself as the spirit world when we perceive it, as Kant's Categorical Imperative implores us to do, as the "Kingdom of Ends." It is not the literal end of the corporeal body that takes us into the spirit world—at least not exclusively. We enter the Kingdom of Ends by dying to the literal perspective. In the same twinkling of an eye that turned the streets of London into the New Jerusalem for Blake, and the city of Dublin into an Homeric archetype of itself for Joyce, the Categorical Imperative transports us to the "Kingdom of Ends." Heaven is not something later, the end for which we use this world as a means. It is, as Jesus put it, already within us. To live in terms of the Categorical Imperative is to live in the Kingdom of a realized eschatology. Start things out in the beginning as you want them to end up in the end. Act as if your every act were to recur eternally [6]. "Act so that you treat humanity . . . always as an

[4] The dream-ego behaves according to the hypothetical imperative and reflects the perspective of egoistic expediency bumbling around in the world of ends.

end and never as a means only" [3, p. 47]. "Heaven and hell/Are one, and here, O terra Infidel" [7, p. 253].

TENNYSON

In his poem, "In Memoriam A. H. H.," Tennyson raises several rhetorical questions in order to give expression to the guilt feelings to which he felt subject during in his bereavement [8, p. 58]:

> Do we indeed desire the dead
> Should still be near us at our side?
> Is there no baseness we would hide?
> No inner vileness that we dread?
>
> Shall he for whose applause I strove,
> I had such reverence for his blame,
> See with clear eyes some hidden shame
> And I be lessened in his love?

Before the angelic presence which his dead friend has obtained through the agency of his own absence Tennyson feels unworthy. He worries that his friend, now freed from the corporeal perspective, will see his "baseness," "inner vileness," and "hidden shame," through the "clear eyes" of death. In expressing these feelings Tennyson is not falling prey to superstitious ideas. Nor is he indulging in parapsychological speculations. The guilt he finds himself subject to is a function of what Hillman has called "the poetic basis of mind" [9, p. xi]. And even the most stalwart of natural scientists may find himself subject to similar poetic sentiments. Again, we must remember our Kant: "The other world is not another place, but only another view."

The guilt particular to bereavement is the result of this change in perspective. Not only do we see our loved ones in their wholeness after death; we see ourselves through their eyes. As Edward Casey, the philosopher of the imagination has suggested, an image, such as Tennyson's dead friend, is not *what* we see, but *how* we see [10].

It is significant that the guilt which the dead friend's image has elicited is almost immediately assuaged by that image as Tennyson continues to explore its imaginal complexity [8, p. 58]:

I wrong the grave with fears untrue.
Shall love be blamed for want of faith?
There must be wisdom with great Death;
The dead shall look me thro' and thro'.

Be near us when we climb or fall;
Ye watch, like God, the rolling hours
With larger other eyes than ours,
To make allowances for us all.

Similia Similibus Curantur

Like cures like. The guilt which Tennyson feels before the image of his dead friend is resolved as he more fully imagines his friend. The unworthiness which he feels when he first recognizes his dead friend as an inhabitant of the Kingdom of Ends is quickly ameliorated when he realizes that his friend, now an inhabitant of the Kingdom of Ends, views him also as an end. The dead who watch over us, Tennyson realizes, are not mean-spirited. All they require of us is the recognition which we failed to grant them in life. Though our guilt and regret may be how the departed loved ones break through to us, the dead have no lasting stake in these emotions. Indeed, we wrong the dead when we relate to them as a means to escape the guilt which they elicit. In the last analysis, guilt is still a projection. But the speck is not in the eye of the dead, the beam is in our own. When guilt is overly noisy or persists too long it may be because the mourner has failed to fully imagine his lost love-object.[5] Although we may recognize ourselves as having fallen from the Kingdom of Ends into the world of means, all we need to attain the Kingdom once more is to adopt the perspective of the Kingdom. If we will but look into the "Eyes [we] dare not meet in dreams" [1, p. 89] deeply enough to see ourselves through them we will be forgiven by them. Our mourning of our lost loved ones is made possible by their mourning of us, a process which turns us from the exploitative.

[5] Hillman writes: "Images are the compelling source of morality and religion as well as the conscientiousness of art. And, as we do not make them up, so we do not make up our response to them, but are 'taught' this response by them as moral instances. It is when we lose the images that we become moralistic, as if the morality contained within the images becomes dissociated, free-floating guilt, a conscience without face" [11, pp. 61-62].

EMMA JUNG

In his autobiography, Jung recounts a dream which he had following his wife's death, a dream "which was like a vision" in that it possessed a certain "objectivity" [12, p. 296].[6]

> [Emma] stood at some distance from me, looking at me squarely. She was in her prime, perhaps about thirty, and wearing the dress which had been made for her many years before by my cousin the medium. It was perhaps the most beautiful thing she had ever worn. Her expression was neither joyful nor sad, but, rather, objectively wise and understanding, without the slightest emotional reaction, as though she were beyond the mist of affects. I knew that it was not she, but a portrait she had commissioned for me. It contained the beginning of our relationship, the events of fifty-three years of marriage, and the end of her life also. Face to face with such wholeness one remains speechless, for it can scarcely be comprehended.

If Jung, unlike Tennyson, did not "wrong the grave with fears untrue" it was because any regrets or guilt feelings he might have felt were instantly ameliorated by the full revelation of his wife's image as an objective image in the Kingdom of Ends. Emma's appearance in Jung's dream—"objectively wise and understanding"—is an example of Tennyson's realization that the dead watch over us "With larger other eyes than ours,/To make allowances for us all." In the Kingdom of Ends guilt is beside the point. It is a fragmentary affect of the fragmentary world. But Emma is no longer fragmented; she is objectively present and whole. Commenting on this experience Jung writes [12, p. 297]:

[6] Following his heart attack in 1944 Jung had a series of visions. Recounting these experiences in his autobiography, he mentions a number of visions relating to the *hieros-gamos*, the mystic or divine marriage. Of these visions he comments: "I would never have imagined that any such experience was possible. It was not a product of imagination. The visions and experiences were utterly real; there was nothing subjective about them; they all had a quality of absolute objectivity" [12, p. 295]. The dream of Emma, according to Jung, was a further experience of this objectivity. In Jung's view he was seeing her objectively, that is, as an essence quite distinct from his projections and emotional ties. When Jung says that these experiences were not products of imagination I believe he means (and here I employ a distinction drawn by Henry Corbin) that they are not imaginary, but rather, real events taking place in the imaginal realm [13].

> The objectivity which I experienced in this dream . . . is part of a completed individuation. It signifies detachment from valuations and from what we call emotional ties. In general, emotional ties are very important to human beings. But they still contain projections, and it is essential to withdraw these projections in order to attain to oneself and to objectivity. Emotional relationships are relationships of desire, tainted by coercion and constraint; something is expected from the other person, and that makes him and ourselves unfree. Objective cognition lies hidden behind the attraction of emotional relationship; it seems to be its central secret. Only through objective cognition is the real *coniunctio* possible.

AN UNDERVALUED PATIENT

Another of Jung's dreams, this time referring to a living person, provides an interesting contrast to his dream of Emma in that it contained a self-reproach and an ethical obligation upon which Jung felt he had to act. In his autobiography, Jung tells of a female patient he worked with whose analysis seemed to bog down and become empty and banal [12, p. 133]. Concerned about this, Jung planned to address this problem in his next session with her. Prior to the session, however, he had a dream which clarified this situation. In his dream, Jung walked through a valley and saw his patient sitting on a balustrade in the highest tower of a castle which was on the top of a steep hill. The woman was so high up that Jung had to bend his head far back to see her. In the morning he awakened with a crick in his neck. Commenting on the dream, Jung writes that its meaning was immediately apparent to him. In life he had for some reason (he does not go into details) been undervaluing his patient—"looking down on her"—and this dream he understood to be working to correct this attitude. At the next session, Jung told the woman his dream and the treatment moved ahead again.

Though Jung did not dream of his woman patient in the fully objectified manner in which he had dreamed of his dead wife, the dream he did have of her corrected a certain subjective bias in him that was interfering with the analysis. True to his belief that "insight into [images] must be converted into an ethical obligation" [12, p. 193], Jung took pains to change his relationship toward his patient to one that more accurately responded to her value. Of course, unlike his dream of Emma, whom he saw "face to face," Jung still saw his patient "through a glass darkly." And yet, the glass through which he perceived his patient—and this is the important point—was somewhat more translucent now. Some of his projections had been withdrawn, some of the veils removed. The relationship was no longer as determined by the emotions it had constellated, and a decisive step closer to the "real *coniunctio*" had been taken. The difference between these two experiences was more one of degree than of kind. Regardless of the fact that Emma was certainly a more significant person to Jung than his patient was, at stake in his relationship with each of them was a recognition of their impersonal significance, the value of each one in and of themselves as essences. The Kantian creed—"act to use humanity . . . always as an end, never simply as a means"—was particularized and brought to bear on his relationship with particular persons by the dreams. Jung's task, whether as husband or as doctor, was to respond to these women as ends. While in the case of Emma, a woman with whom Jung no longer conducted a relationship in the world of means, nothing more was required beyond a recognition of the "central secret" that his marriage to her, far from being over, was continuing to consummate itself in the "real *coniunctio*" of "objective cognition," in the case of his patient, a woman whom he was very much connected with in the world of means, Jung felt an ethical obligation to change his attitude and behavior toward her such that the analysis might more congruently resemble the Kingdom of Ends.

FROM FALSE GUILT TO TRUE GUILT

As psychotherapists and bereavement counsellors well know, the bereaved are frequently subject to self-reproaches that at first appear to be inane and ridiculous. Long after a loved one has died, the bereaved survivor continues to ruminate about things that might have prevented the death. "If only I had not asked him to do that errand," laments a bereft spouse. "Why didn't I give her her pills earlier," a widower asks himself for the thousandth time, despite the fact that the doctor has assured him that his wife's death was the result of entirely different causes.

Self-help books normalize this kind of self-recrimination. They identify guilt-feelings as a common feature of mourning and relate them to the need to deny loss and retain control even if only by clutching at straws. Though these accounts are, doubtless, partly true, guilt rarely surrenders to the reassurance it elicits, nor is it easily explained away. On the contrary, it is precisely those guilt-feelings that seem the most ludicrous and that we think could be relieved with common sense and kindness that prove to be the most incorrigible. What is it that the psyche wants of the guilt-ridden mourner? What is it the dead want?

In his paper, "Notes Upon a Case of Obsessional Neurosis," Freud suggests that "When there is a *mesalliance* . . . between an affect [such as guilt] and the occasion for it," the physician should not contest the guilty verdict which the patient levels against himself, but, rather, look for its true background [14, p. 313]. In marked contrast to the layman, who would deduce from the discrepancy between the intensity of the guilt-feelings and the trivial content of the associated ruminations that the guilt is exaggerated, the physician, in Freud's view, considers the "affect [to be] justified." As Freud explains,

> The sense of guilt cannot in itself be further criticized. But it belongs to another content, which is unknown (*unconscious*), and which requires to be looked for. The known ideational content has only got into its actual position owing to a mistaken association [14, pp. 313-314].

The following case example illustrates Freud's insight into the legitimacy of the odd guilt-feelings which the bereaved may suffer. However, in contrast to Freud's subsequent step of referring them to the repressed passions of the Oedipus-complex, we shall refer them to the Categorical Imperative instead.

A young woman, the mother of two children under two, and the wife of a husband who physically and verbally abused her, was referred to me for therapy by her doctor who was concerned about her depression and suicidal ideation. In the initial interview she told me about her husband's drunken binges, the children's needs, her great emptiness, and, most important, her unrelenting sense of guilt. What was it she felt guilty about? Three years ago, shortly before she married, her grandfather had died. Though she had visited him frequently during his illness, she had been on a date with her future husband, not at her grandfather's bedside, at the moment of the old man's death. Though friends had tried to help her with these guilt-feelings by reminding her that she had been a good grand-daughter and that he had been unconscious in those hours preceding death and, therefore, would not have known whether she was there or not, she had continued from that time to the present to vex herself with self-reproaches.

Sensing that the two problems might be related I asked the woman what her grandfather would think of her present marital situation. Would he with whom she had had the good fortune to experience a relationship of mutual love, trust, support and respect be proud of her in her current life? Would he who related to her "as an end never simply as a means" not reproach her for allowing herself to be misused by her husband? My questions hit the mark. What had appeared to be false guilt on deeper scrutiny proved to be true guilt. The young woman was guilty—and of the very thing she had accused herself: dating in the world of means and betraying, thereby, the Categorical Imperative of her grandfather's love. By accepting and deepening her awareness of her guilt, the therapy restored her to her grandfather. To be cured of her guilt, I told her, she must accept it and make amends. Though she had not been with her grandfather at his death, she must live as if he were with her now. Only her grandfather could help her to sort out what to do about her marriage. He had taught her much about self-esteem.

Though this woman's bereavement guilt began shortly after her grandfather's death, its source was not the event of his actual passing three years ago. On the contrary, it was something that she had been re-inventing for herself each day by living against that side of herself that her grandfather had reflected. Mourning is as concerned with the ongoing life of the living as with the past life of the dead. Indeed, as in this illustration, the difficulties which the bereaved may appear to have untangling themselves from the dead may, on closer scrutiny, be shown to be a difficulty in creatively living their actual, ongoing life. The dead with whom the patient is preoccupied may be metaphorical of the problem in the current life, which is not being lived adequately.

THE SUPER-EGO REIMAGINED

Freud believed that the guilt feelings to which we are all subject can be derived, at least in part, from a loss that we have not personally experienced. This loss, which Freud considered to be common to all mankind, was the result of a parricide committed in pre-historic times. According to Freud's 'reconstruction' of this event, a *construction* based upon his reading of Frazer's *Totemism and Exogamy* and Smith's *Religion of the Semites* as well as the "archaic vestiges" in his patient's dreams and fantasies, early man lived in family clans which were "under the domination of a single, powerful, violent and jealous male" [15, p. 129]. This dominant male—Freud calls him the "Primal father"—possessed all the women in a horde for himself and drove his sons away. One day, however, the brothers united together, over-powered the father and killed him. Having vented their aggressive instincts, they then became subject to remorse, for they also loved their father. Unable to mourn their loss, the brothers created in themselves a Super-ego by means of identification, thereby creating the "restrictions which should prevent a repetition of the deed" [16, p. 120].

If the family clan over which the Primal Father tyrannized was the psychoanalytic counterpart to the Garden of Eden, the killing of the father, in Freud's view, was the original sin to which each successive generation down to the present is subject. Each of us, in other words, is subject to the same ambivalence of emotion as were the brothers whom the father had expelled from the horde. The difference, however, is that we are *a priori* subject to the guilt which our ancient forebears created by giving full reign to their aggressive instinct. Due to the manner in which the Primal Father continues to haunt our psychic life, there is an increased likelihood that the aggressive instinct, which revives anew in each generation, will be inhibited. The more aggression we inhibit and the more pleasure we renounce, the more powerful the Super-ego becomes. This ever-increasing sense of guilt is the by-product of the progress of civilization, for Freud, and is responsible for many of its discontents [16, p. 114].

> Every renunciation then becomes a dynamic fount of conscience; every fresh abandonment of gratification increases its severity and intolerance . . . every impulse of aggression which we omit to gratify is taken over by the super-ego and goes to heighten its aggressiveness (against the ego).

We are judged, according to Freud, by the very impulses which we have inhibited or renounced. Far from preventing guilt, our attempts to evade the affect actually increase it. What we give up as Id punishes us as Super-ego. Guilt is a part of us, an institution within the psyche. We are damned if we do and damned if we don't. Worse: the core of the guilt-complex is utterly irrational and amoral. In contrast to other thinkers such as Jung, Neumann or Buber, Freud does not consider conscience to bear any necessary relationship to ethics.

Commenting on Freud's theory of neurosis, Jung writes [17, p. 420]:

> Freud makes his theory of neurosis—so admirably suited to the nature of neurotics—much too dependent on the neurotic ideas from which precisely the patients suffer. This leads to the pretence (which suits the neurotic down to the ground) that the *causa efficiens* of his neurosis lies in the remote past. In reality the neurosis is manufactured anew every day, with the help of a false

> attitude that consists in the neurotic's thinking and feeling as he does and justifying it by his theory of neurosis.

These comments are just as true in our present context. Freud's analysis of guilt provides a brilliant, if unwitting, account of how guilt accumulates as a consequence of the failure to elegize a loss. Like his theory of the etiology of neurosis, his theory of guilt is "too dependent on the neurotic ideas from which precisely the patients suffer." By locating the source of guilt in the past, Freud replicates in his theory the falsifying attitude which manufactures our guilt anew each day. *Totem and Taboo, Civilization and Its Discontents, Moses and Monotheism*: it is as if Freud stopped writing these elegies at the point at which his guilt feelings became activated—unaware that these works were in fact elegies. Contrary to Tennyson, who was absolved from the guilt which the image of his dead friend elicited by continuing to elaborate that image, and contrary to Jung, who stood guiltless before the fully articulated image of his dead wife, Freud infers the existence of a Super-ego. The problem here is that the concept of the super-ego is not an image and therefore cannot heal or be healed. The concept of the Super-ego locates the source of our guilt feelings in a generic, no-name loss—our great, great, infinitely great grandfather. Like a patient trying to evade an unwelcome affect, the concept of the super-ego is a defense against guilt. Far from being the seat of conscience, it is simply what guilt becomes when we fail to imagine into it. It could be argued, of course, that Freud's story of the murder of the father constitutes an imaginal account of loss and guilt. The problem with Freud's account, however, is that it is monolithic, and unspecific. One imaginal story underpins all loss. But the Primal Father of Freud's theory is not the shade which haunts our guilt—at least not if we imagine our losses precisely. "Primal Father" is merely the image which Freud, the epic elegist, assigned to the multitude of losses and guilts which mankind has failed to imagine or mourn. Civilization, in Freud's accounting of it, is a failed mourning process. As a species, Mankind is cultured more by the losses he has identified with than by the losses he has imagined and mourned. Each experience of guilt which we fail to embody in an image combines with a multitude of other disembodied guilts to become that free-floating sense of guilt and lost innocence which Freud referred to with the reifying term Super-ego. But the problem is not our guilty deeds, or our guilty feelings, it is our avoidance of guilt. As Martin Buber puts it [cited in 18, p. 177]:

> Anyone who rids himself of this guilt gets into the deficiency of sickness because of *not wanting* to be guilty. He does not heed the voice of conscience calling him to *be* guilty. But the continually unfulfilled and unfulfillable call to *be* guilty is unendurable. Consequently guiltiness turns into *feeling* guilty and the call of conscience into punishment, while guilt itself becomes a demonstrative symptom of being hindered, a demonstration of the "inability" to follow the call of conscience. And yet what alone matters is that life should be lived from the fact of guilt, not indeed as a life of expiation, but rather of at-one-ment, a life that makes amends, that makes good."

Guilt, for Buber, is more than a feeling. It is an ontological condition of being apart from God. To put it in more Kantian terms, guilt is a function of the discrepancy between the world of means and the Kingdom of Ends. When we experience ourselves as being guilty we are seeing ourselves, to some degree, from the "other world." What Freud called Super-ego, on the other hand, corresponds to what Buber calls "*not wanting* to be guilty." In order not to feel guilty we do all sorts of things—deny we are our brother's keeper, plead guilty to lesser crimes than we have actually committed, punish ourselves with the "deficiency of sickness," blame others. But if what we do out of guilt is only done in order to evade or expiate guilt feelings we will again be in violation of the Categorical Imperative. It is in precisely this sense that the Super-ego—that psychoanalytic entity which guilt becomes when it is evaded—comes into being.

The particular relationship to guilt which psychoanalysis calls "Super-ego" is the psychoanalytic analogue of hell. Like Kant's spirit world, this hell of the Super-ego is not a place, but a perspective. Just as we enter the Kingdom of Ends by imagining events in terms of their teleological perspective, we assign ourselves to the hell of the Super-ego by attempting to evade the Kingdom's call to *be* guilty. But if we can accept the fact of ourselves being guilty we can then adjust ourselves to the heavenly order which has called us to *be* guilty. This adjustment to the images which animate our guilt corresponds to what Buber calls, "at-one-ment, a life that makes amends. . . . " If, on the other hand, we attempt to repress the call to *be* guilty through an evasion of guilt feelings—Buber speaks of a "life of expiation"—we cut ourselves off from the mercy which is an inherent part of the affect's imaginal background.

What the patient needs to realize is that the image which underpins his guilt, the image which "calls him to *be* guilty," is *not* that "single, powerful, violent and jealous male" which Freud called the Primal Father. The objective correlative of this image, if such a correlative exists at all, may be the harsh parental treatment which has taught the children of every generation from the dawn of time to be afraid to be guilty. As Freud puts it, ". . . the Super-ego, has retained essential features of the introjected [parents], namely, their power, their severity, their tendency to watch over and to punish" [19, p. 264]. We quote Freud here against himself in order to draw a crucial distinction. The Super-ego is not the source of guilt; it is a repository of the patient's fear of guilt. Fearful of being guilty, the patient wrongly attributes a severity to guilt which is foreign to it. Years of being punished by the inhabitants of the world of means makes him fearful to admit to himself the guilt which calls him to the Kingdom of Ends.[7] In therapy, the patient's fear of guilt must be explored and differentiated from the guilt itself in order that he may be helped to heed the call to *be* guilty. The images which the call to *be* guilty calls the patient to recognize are hidden well behind his fear of being punished for being wrong. In order for the patient to be healed of his guilt by his guilt the therapist must help him to dethrone that Super-ego or Primal Father who contaminates guilt with the fear of being harmed and who has presided from time immemorial over the lowest form of morality.

THE EGO-IDEAL

Having differentiated guilt from the Super-ego, we must now differentiate it from what Freud called the ego-ideal. In Freud's view, we are measured not only by the Super-ego; we are measured as well by an internal representation of the "narcissistic perfection" which we had to renounce as we grew up [21, p. 51].

> To this ideal ego is . . . directed the self-love which the real ego enjoyed in childhood. The narcissism seems to be now displaced on to this new ideal ego, which, like the infantile ego, deems itself the possessor of all perfections. As always where the libido is concerned, here again man has shown himself incapable of giving up a gratification he has once enjoyed. He is not willing to forego his

[7] Freud uses the term "Categorical Imperative" erroneously in connection with the Super-ego: "As the child was once under a compulsion to obey its parents, so the ego submits to the categorical imperative of its super-ego" [19, p. 38]. The Categorical Imperative, of course, has nothing to do with the Super-ego. Strictly speaking, behaving as directed by the Super-ego would correspond to the Hypothetical Imperative.

> narcissistic perfection in his childhood; and if, as he develops, he is disturbed by the admonitions of others and his own critical judgement is awakened, he seeks to recover the early perfection, thus wrested from him, in the new form of an ego-ideal. That which he projects ahead of him as his ideal is merely his substitute for the lost narcissism of his childhood—the time when he was his own ideal.

The polymorphously perverse child, which supposedly would have been spoilt had the rod of the Super-ego been spared, is simply irrepressible. The narcissism which we concede to the Super-ego survives in the form of a projection upon the future, an orienting ideal. Though we have been expelled from the Garden of Eden by the punishing gods of our childhood, we may be admitted to the New Jerusalem if we become as little children once more. Once the ego-ideal has been established in the Super-ego, it too can play a supervisory role in mental life. It too can take on the "severity of the father," and with his switch insist that the ego regain the pleasures that the parents had demanded it forsake. The task to which the ego-ideal calls us is the same task Coleridge saw as belonging to the poet: carrying the "feelings of childhood into the powers of Manhood." Failure to actualize in life the childhood values which have been enshrined in the ego-ideal results in a diminished sense of accomplishment, a sense of having let ourselves down.

The ego-ideal is important to our discussion of bereavement guilt because of the role it has played in some cases in the making of the original object-choices of the bereaved. According to Freud, we frequently fall in love with people who personify for us our ego-ideal. This tendency, Freud believed [20, p. 142], is particularly evident in cases where there exists an overvaluation of a loved person, such that this person is immune to criticism and is valued in all the particularities of his or her character more highly than people who are not loved [22, p. 143]:

> The tendency which falsifies judgement in this respect is that of *idealization*. . . . the object is being treated in the same way as our own ego, so that when we are in love a considerable amount of narcissistic libido overflows on to the object. It is even obvious, in many forms of love-choice, that the object serves as a substitute for some unattained ego ideal of our own. We love it on account of the perfections which we have striven to reach for our own ego, and which we should now like to procure in this roundabout way as a means of satisfying our narcissism.

When a love-object which was overvalued, or better, incorrectly valued, as a substitute for unattained ego ideals dies, it is the loss of the ego ideal, not the loss of the love-object him- or herself which the bereaved survivor mourns. After the divorce or even the death, the bereaved may feel as if his or her own life was a failure. Without the living proximity to the dead partner, the bereaved survivor may feel cut off from the idealism which that partner embodied, and become demoralized. Alternatively, the dead loved one may be lionized and sentimentalized (rather than accurately imagined) in order that he or she may continue to represent the survivor's ego-ideal from beyond the grave.

The mourning process reflects the quality of the love process. Matches that were made in the world of means tend to be mourned in the world of means as well. If the otherness of the lover was never recognized in life, it may be difficult to recognize in death as well—*even though this recognition in that last of meeting places is what the mourning process is all about.*

"So act to use humanity in your own person and in the person of every other, always at the same time as an end, never simply as a means." When our love process and mourning process have merely been a "roundabout . . . means of satisfying our narcissism," both are in violation of the Categorical Imperative. In therapy the patient must be helped to recognize the otherness of each lost love-object. He must be helped to see that the death of the love-object is not simply a wound to his own ideal identity; it is an individuating act on the part of the deceased. If the patient can come to see this and reproach himself for his true sin of having used the love-object as a means to narcissistic satisfaction, he may at last enter the perspective of the Kingdom of Ends, the Kingdom of a true, as distinct from narcissistic, love.

DEATH'S DREAM KINGDOM

What Eliot in "The Hollow Men" calls "death's dream kingdom," and what Kant in *The Critique of Practical Reason* calls the "Kingdom of Ends," is the true background of guilt. Like original sin, guilt is an ontological condition, a state of being which is incongruent with Being in the larger meaning of that term. We feel guilty because we are not whole and have not been relating to the wholeness of others. The Greek word for "sin," *hamartia*, signifies "missing the mark," as when an arrow misses its target. The call to *be* guilty is a call to get back on target. Guilt reminds us that we should aim for the "ends" of things. It implies a shift in perspective. We see our actions as if from another world of values. Time gives way to eternity. We consider our lives from a more final point of view. What if this action were to be my last action? What if I should never get another opportunity to acknowledge her value? Has my way of being-in-the-world been congruent with the other world of which we are also member?

In the deepest sense, guilt is a function of the discrepancy between our life and our death—and that may be another reason why we try to evade it. We evade guilt in order to avoid the perspective of death which guilt brings home to us so personally. Not willing to imagine a meaning for our lives against the background of life's one great certainty, death, we defer death's teleological sense of morality to the literal end of our lives, not realizing that a Last Judgement at that point may be too late to do us any good. In bereavement, however, death is difficult to deny, and we find ourselves more vulnerable to the specific guilts that have become associated with its neglected perspective. A loved one has died and through his death has become wholly an end in himself. We see him in his subtle body. We see him as he had died trying to be seen. He is now a full-time resident in "death's dream kingdom," and by continuing to appear to us in the mind, he reminds us that we are part-time residents of that kingdom as well.

"If only I had been home I could have prevented his death." "If only I had known he was so depressed." "If only I'd beheld him in the spirit in the first place." At first we feel remorse about the death as a physical event. Even when the death was from natural causes or due to an accident we feel it to have been a function of our neglect. "If only we had been there!" we exclaim. This sentiment is absurd only from the point of view of the world of means. From the perspective of the Kingdom of Ends, however, it is quite appropriate. The guilt brings home to us the extent to which we were not there. The soul-making that we did not do weighs heavily upon our hearts. We regret that we missed out on the poetry of our loved ones, expecting only prose. Why did we not recognize sooner the manner in which Great Death has always made his darkness beautiful in them?

The bereaved become morbidly fixated in regret only if they fail to realize that their regret is a form of recognition and therefore its own cure. Gradually, the "if only" which ties the regret to a past which the dead no longer inhabit must give way to a recognition of the present imaginal relationship which underpins it. Without regret there could be no recognition. Without recognition, no regret. The important thing is that we make the guilt into images, or better, find the images in the guilt so that we may at last come into immediate contact with the angelic essences of our love. Forgiveness is not really the point. The sin which must be atoned is the sin of our respective omission. "In this last of meeting places" the moral imperative is simply this: that we finally meet one another. In the final analysis, getting here is all that counts.

REFERENCES

1. T. S. Eliot, *Collected Poems 1909-1962*, Faber & Faber, London, 1974.
2. D. Runes (ed.), *Dictionary of Philosophy*, Littlefield, Adams, Totowa, 1962.
3. I. Kant, *Foundations of the Metaphysics of Morals*, L. W. Beck (trans.), Bobbs-Merrill, Indianapolis, 1959.
4. A. Jaffe, *Apparitions: An Archetypal Approach to Death Dreams and Ghosts*, Spring Publications, Dallas, 1978.
5. H. Corbin, *Avicenna and the Visionary Recital*, Spring Publications, Dallas, 1980.
6. F. Nietzsche, *Thus Spoke Zarathustra*, R. Hollingdale (trans.), Penguin Books, Harmondsworth, 1961.
7. W. Stevens, Esthetique du Mal, in *The Palm at the End of the Mind: Selected Poems and a Play*, H. Stevens (ed.), Random House, New York, 1972.
8. A. Tennyson, In Memoriam A. H. H., in *Victorian Poetry and Poetics*, second edition, W. E. Houghton and G. R. Strange (eds.), Houghton Mifflin, Boston, 1968.
9. J. Hillman, *Re-Visioning Psychology*, Harper & Row, New York, 1975.
10. E. Casey, Toward a Phenomenology of Imagination, *The Journal of the British Society of Phenomenology*, Vol. 5, 1974.
11. J. Hillman, *Healing Fiction*, Station Hill, Barrytown, 1983.
12. C. G. Jung, *Memories, Dreams, Reflections*, A. Jaffe (ed.), R. & C. Winston (trans.), Random House, New York, 1961.
13. H. Corbin, Mundus Imaginalis or the Imaginary and the Imaginal, in *Spring: An Annual of Archetypal Psychology and Jungian Thought*, Spring Publications, Dallas, 1972.
14. S. Freud, Notes Upon a Case of Obsessional Neurosis, in *Collected Papers*, Vol. III, A. & J. Strachey (trans.), Hogarth Press and the Institute of Psycho-Analysis, 1950.
15. S. Freud, *An Autobiographical Study*, J. Strachey (trans.), W. W. Norton, New York, 1963.
16. S. Freud, *Civilization and Its Discontents*, The Hogarth Press, London, 1949.
17. C. G. Jung, *Symbols of Transformation, Collected Works*, Vol. 5, R. F. C. Hull (Trans.), Princeton University Press, Princeton, 1967.

18. E. Blum, Freud and Conscience, in *Conscience,* The Curatorium of the C. G. Jung Institute (eds.), Northwestern University Press, Evanston, 1970.
19. S. Freud, The Economic Problem in Masochism, in *Collected Papers,* Vol. II, R. Riviere (trans.), Hogarth Press and the Institute of Psychoanalysis, 1950.
20. S. Freud, *The Ego and the Id,* J. Riviere (trans.), W. W. Norton, New York, 1962.
21. S. Freud, On Narcissism: An Introduction, in *Collected Papers,* Vol. VI, R. Riviere (trans.), Hogarth Press and the Institute of Psychoanalysis, 1950.
22. S. Freud, Group Psychology and the Analysis of the Ego, in *The Pelican Freud Library,* Vol. 12, J. Strachey (trans.), Penguin Books, Harmondsworth, 1985.

CHAPTER 6

Elegiac Dreaming

> . . . the interesting part of love is usually its decay, that is, the impossibility. When it falls apart, when it doesn't work, when all the pathologies appear (and aren't disguised in bliss). You see this decay in dreams when the old lovers don't want each other any more, when an old attraction, an old pattern doesn't work. And then you are haunted by them, the old figures, for years afterward. They return like ghosts. The eros is getting psychized. Then you have something very painful but very interesting to work with. What are these ghosts returning for [1, p. 180]?
>
> James Hillman

TWO KINDS OF DREAMS

An imaginal approach to the mourning process pays particular attention to dreams. Whether these dreams are to be considered a function of the psychodynamics of the bereaved survivor or a function of the on-going imaginal life of the lost object is a question of the greatest practical importance to both. Jung's statement—"In the deepest sense we all dream not *out of ourselves*, but out of what lies *between us and the other*" [2, p. 172]—is true as well of the dreams which lie between us and those absent others whom we call the dead. The loss of a loved one—whether through death or separation—is not a loss of being but a shift in it. The ontological assumptions which are required to mourn lost objects are subtler and more complex than the ontological assumptions that had underpinned our previous relationship with them. The mourning process is paradoxical. Although our loved ones are "gone," we can only find *in them* the wherewithal to let them go. Without the help of the dead themselves the mourning process would become sequestered in grief. But in death's dream kingdom there is a funeral which the dead conduct for themselves. Although the bereaved are invited, the dead write their own elegies. As Eliot put it in "Little Gidding" [3, p. 222]:

> We die with the dying:
> See, they depart, and we go with them.
> We are born with the dead:
> See, they return and bring us with them.
> The moment of the rose and the moment of the yew-tree
> Are of equal duration.

Of the dreams which present the imaginal background of the mourning process two types may be distinguished. On the one hand, we may group together those dreams which place particular emphasis on the grief of the bereaved. Characteristic of these dreams is a focus on the *attachment relationship* between the bereaved survivor and the lost loved one *as the lost loved one was known historically*. Some dreams within this group seem to be mere wish-fulfillments. The dream-ego communes with the lost object as if there had been no loss at all. In other dreams, especially when it would be possible to resume a relationship that has been ambivalently renounced (i.e. separation or divorce), the lost loved one may appear in an ambiguous manner—attractive one moment, repulsive the next. And again, still within this group, belong those dreams where the dream-ego and the lost object appear in a manner which is metaphoric of each other's sorrow. Here *pathos* is evoked, and the therapist empathizes.

On the other hand, we may group together those dreams which seem to explore the on-going imaginal life of the lost love-object. These dreams usually come as a surprise. The lost love-object appears in a novel aspect. In the imaginal world of the dream, it lives, moves, and has its being in a manner quite indifferent to the grief of the bereaved. The personalistic emotions of the bereaved dream-ego are eclipsed by the ahistorical appearance of the lost love-object. There is an unveiling. The contingency of life falls away. What had once seemed arbitrary reveals itself as essence. The image ceases to be a function of our desires. Desire itself becomes imaginal, reflected now in the mirror of the free soul.

While pure examples of both these kinds of dreams are not uncommon, it is more often the case that a dream may juggle both concerns—grief *and* elegy, sentimentality *and* vision, remembered impressions *and* "the images that yet/Fresh images beget."

The dreams which follow were dreamt by a man who had renounced a highly valued relationship, which he had come to realize was at odds with his larger life. Though he dearly loved his partner of six years, he was also convinced of the necessity of leaving her so that they could each pursue the possibilities of life which they had been sacrificing to their relationship. During the first year of the separation the dreamer experienced periods of intense ambivalence. Occasionally, he even did an about-face and re-contacted his lover. But each time he did so he was soon more persuaded than before that the parting would have to be final, even though it was a parting in love. Although he did not formulate it in this way, the dreamer's renunciation of his relationship to his lover was congruent with Kant's Categorical Imperative. Attempts to change the style of the relationship were not sufficient. In order to treat himself and her "always at the same time as an end, never simply as a means" he came to realize he had to end the relationship, for what he did not know.

DREAM ONE

> Evelyn is with me. She is naked. Beneath her nipples on each breast is another nipple. I realize these second nipples are cancerous tumors. On her body the skin has grown many other tumors that look like mouths. (The skin in these places looks like lips formed into a kiss.) They are parted and the white core suggests teeth. I want to make it all better. I want to enter into relationship with her again to make it all better. There is a deep sorrow.

This dream, a dream typical of that group which reflect the *grief* of the mourning process, depicts in precise images the sense of sorrow which the dreamer feels. Evelyn's body, covered with cancerous tumors which are like nipples and mouths, images the pathologizing of the tender love tie that had previously united her with the dreamer. The very places where the kisses of love had once been placed have now been kissed by death. The image is reminiscent of a passage from Yeats' poem, "The Sorrow of Love": "A girl arose that had red mournful lips/And seemed the greatness of the world in tears, . . ." The dreamer's pain is very great. Empathic mirroring by the therapist of the dreamer's misery and dejection was necessary to help him to bear his grief. It may also have helped the Evelyn-figure by relieving her of the burden of having to reflect the dreamer's grief. All this took time. It was a bitter process.

The dream-ego, moved by the woesome Evelyn of his dream, "wants to make it all better" by "enter[ing] into relationship with her again." As in their previous love-making, there is now in this death-making or soul-making process a loss of boundaries. The dream-ego wishes to fuse with the dream-Evelyn. To put it in the language of psychoanalysis, the dreamer, having regressed to the organizational level of the oral stage (mouth, teeth, nipples), incorporates the lost object into itself. Freud writes [4, p. 18]:

> We succeeded in explaining the painful disorder of melancholia by supposing that an object which was lost has been set up again inside the ego—that is, that an object-cathexis has been replaced by an identification. . . . [T]his kind of substitution has a great share in determining the form taken by the ego and . . . makes an essential contribution towards building up what is called its 'character.'

Although the dreamer has renounced his relationship with Evelyn, the mortified libidinal trends that bound him to her have become identified with her. No longer the object of desire, Evelyn is now the image within which desire works. Of course, the waking ego, moved by the dream, may try to act the dream out in the world. The dreamer may confuse the dream's Evelyn with the real woman and call her up to resuscitate their old union, as opposed to resurrecting an imaginal one. But if the dreamer can stay with the dream, the grief it contains will gradually be transformed by the images which there make mourning possible. Bit by bit, the "transformation of [the] erotic object-choice into an alteration of the ego," according to our re-visioned reading of Freud, will allow the ego to "obtain control over the id and deepen its relations with it—at the cost, it is true, of acquiescing to a large extent in the id's experiences" [4, p. 20]. This last phrase—"acquiescing to a large extent in the id's experiences"—is important. Although "the transformation of object-libido into narcissistic libido . . . obviously implies an abandonment of sexual aims, a desexualization" [4, p. 20], *the ego's relationship to desire itself is deepened*. The mourning process does not simply desexualize desire, it *deliteralizes* it. The *energy* of the libido is not lost;

it is transformed. As the mourning process goes on love become increasingly imaginal.

DREAM TWO

> We are near a huge body of water, on a concrete pier. Evelyn has dinner plates that have pictures painted on them. I'm not pictured on these plates as frequently as I'd like. Some are bright and colorful. Others are dull and porous. These ones let the juices of the food in and thus are dirty in the same way a cutting board is dirty. They have a pungent, earthy smell to them like a mother's body. These plates, being of little value in themselves, have the virtue that they can be smashed like plates in Greek restaurants.

Again, in this dream, there is a stress on orality (plates, juices of food, cutting board) and reference is made to the infantile prototype of the bonding relationship ("a pungent, earthy smell . . . like a mother's body"). By "a body of water, on a concrete pier," the dream-ego is being served a little supper of loss. From the archetypal point of view, the water's edge is an appropriate setting for such a meal. Not only is the water's edge rich in reveries of death (Charon, Ophelia) and parting (Dido and Aeneas), it contains both in a maternal embrace. As Jung put it, the "black waters of death are [also] the waters of life, for death with its cold embrace is the maternal womb, just as the sea devours the sun but brings it forth again" [5, p. 218]. The very process that detaches the dreamer from his personal love-object, attaches him to the collective unconscious, connects him to the sea. The mourning process regresses to those elemental levels of the psyche which are deep enough to contain it. What Freud wrote of as "the transformation of object-libido into narcissistic libido . . . ," "an abandonment of sexual aims, a desexualization" and an "acquiescing to a large extent in the id's experiences" is here enacting itself mythopoeically. As Jung put it in a chapter called, "The Sacrifice," in his book, *Symbols of Transformation* [5, pp. 419-420]:

> The regressing libido apparently desexualizes itself by retreating back step by step to the presexual stage of earliest infancy. Even there it does not make a halt, but in a manner of speaking continues right back to the intrauterine, prenatal condition and, leaving the sphere of personal psychology altogether, irrupts into the collective psyche where Jonah saw the "mysteries" ("representations collectives") in the whale's belly. The libido thus reaches

> a kind of inchoate condition in which, like Theseus and Peirithoüs on their journey to the underworld, it may easily stick fast. But it can also tear itself loose from the maternal embrace and return to the surface with new possibilities of life.

What Jung refers to as the "mysteries" which Jonah saw in the belly of the whale corresponds to the images which the Evelyn-figure shows to the dream-ego on the concrete pier by the water's edge. Significantly, the dream-ego finds that he is "not pictured on these plates as frequently as [he would] like." This is because, as we just heard from Jung, he is "leaving the sphere of personal psychology. . . ." Though some of the plates are painted with images which are "bright and colorful" (the dreamer associated these images with the happy, sentimental images of Evelyn and himself which he had in his photograph album), other plates are "dull and porus." The dull, porous plates cannot hold bright, colorful images. On the contrary, images seep into them like the juices of food into a cutting board. These plates are deeper. Their pungent, maternal smell reaches "back to the intrauterine, prenatal condition." They present the collective psyche. The dreamer is served his personal loss on plates saturated with the juices of a multitude of severed attachments.

At the end of the dream it is stated that the dull, porous plates, "being of little value, have the virtue that they can be smashed like plates in a Greek restaurant." As in the Greek custom, the dishes may be smashed because the feast is sacred. No one else can use them. Part of absorbing the experience of having renounced or lost a loved one is digesting the fact that the relationship is irrepeatable. At this point the dreamer was invited to share, in a celebratory spirit, some of what he cherished, and would therefore miss, about his relationship with Evelyn.

Inasmuch as the microcosm of our lives is contained within a cultural macrocosm, the grief which the dream-ego and the dream Evelyn taste in this phase of the mourning process can be compared to the grief of the Last Supper. As in that feast of sacrifice, though on a more mundane level, the dream-figures bid farewell to their love, thereby allowing it to fulfill its greater mission in the psyche. No longer will communion (or what the lovers as inhabitants of the world of means had confused for communion) happen in the flesh. On the contrary, as the Evelyn-figure becomes increasingly discontinuous with the feelings and assumptions which had underpinned the dreamer's earthly grasp of Evelyn, his perception of Evelyn (the actual woman) will be freed from the "mist of affects" and come to approximate more closely, if only in the form of a meaningful parting, what Jung called "the real coniunctio" [5, p. 297].

The smashing of the porous plates into which the libido has seeped (nekyia motif) has another meaning as well. The danger that the libido, having regressed to an inchoate condition, might become fixated there, as did Theseus and Peirithous on their journey to the underworld, appears to be surmounted. The dream's suggestion that the plates can be broken suggests that the libido which they reflect and contain can "tear itself loose from the maternal embrace and return to the surface with new possibilities for life." It need only die to live again. As D. H. Lawrence writes in his poem, "The Ship of Death" [6, p. 2513]:

> We are dying, we are dying, so all we can do
> is now be willing to die, and to build the ship
> of death to carry the soul on the longest journey.
>
> A little ship, with oars and food
> and little dishes, and all accouterments
> fitting and ready for the departing soul.
> Now launch the small ship, now as the body dies
> and life departs, launch out, the fragile soul
> in the fragile ship of courage, the ark of faith
> with its store of food and little cooking pans
> and changes of clothes,
> upon the flood's back waste
> upon the waters of the end
> upon the sea of death. . . .

DREAM THREE

I am with Evelyn. Her skin is very white—unnaturally so. We sit on a street corner at night. To my surprise I notice she is naked. She sits with her legs drawn up into her arms with her head resting on her knees. She looks like that pencil sketch by Van Gogh of his destitute friend, a prostitute, the sketch titled "Sorrow." I point out to her that she is naked, anxiously indicating to her that she should cover herself. But she is not naked. She has a tube top on and a pair of shorts. It is only the way she was sitting that made me think she was naked. As she unfolds herself, catapulting to a standing position, she righteously declares that she is clothed. Then we are back at my parents' house in the driveway. I watch Evelyn and Terry

> clean snow off a car and get in. The car is a time-machine car like the one in the Spielberg film, "Back to the Future." They are going "back to the future."

While the earlier dreams in this series were more concerned with the grief of the mourning process, this dream places more emphasis on the on-going imaginal life of the Evelyn-figure. Though the dream-ego attempts to cover the dream-Evelyn's forlorn nakedness at the beginning of the dream with his pity and concern, she quickly differentiates herself from his image of her. She is *not* a destitute prostitute like the one Van Gogh sketched. Nor is she sorrowful. The dream-ego has misperceived her. Catapulting to a standing position, the Evelyn-figure reveals herself in a new and surprising fashion. As an imaginal being in her own right, she is radically discontinuous with the dream-ego's assumptions about her. Perceiving her as a down-and-out whore in need of compassionate help (Van Gogh took the prostitute he sketched into his home) is merely a defense against her autonomy. The dream-ego must realize that the Evelyn-figure is not his personal property. As a subtle body she has overcome the gravity of his attachment to her. She is no longer willing to be confined to the static role of being his faithful introject.

The unnatural whiteness of the dream-Evelyn's skin points to the *albedo* phase of the alchemical process. The *nigredo* blackness of the first two dreams has given way. Soul has been extracted from the body. The putrid prose of grief has given way to the poetry of a subtler body. *Imagination* has become as flesh. Though there may still be more attachments to mortify, some have already been whitened into psyche. The Evelyn-figure is now an image, or better said, an angel. Though the mourning process is normal, it is not natural. Like the alchemical process, it is an *opus contra naturam*, a work against nature into culture.

The scene changes. The dream-ego looks on as Evelyn and an old girlfriend, Terry, clean the snow off a time-machine car which is parked in his parents' driveway. Commenting on this part of the dream, the dreamer added that he had the impression that Terry had driven it there from the spirit world in order to pick up Evelyn and take her back with her. The white snow on the car was not natural snow: it was the white, snowy dust of the spirit world.

Clearly, the Evelyn-figure is passing over into another order. Terry, an old girlfriend of the dreamer's has come to take her to that place outside time ("back to the future") where she now resides. That it is an old girlfriend that escorts the Evelyn-figure to the other world makes poetic sense. As Eliot put it [6, p. 2554]:

> No poet, no artist of any art [including, we may add, the art of relationship, the art of love] has his complete meaning alone. His significance, his appreciation is the appreciation of his relation to the dead poets and artists. You cannot value him alone; you must set him, for contrast and comparison, among the dead.

It is precisely because Terry was once the dreamer's lover that she comes for Evelyn. Their proximity to one another is part of the valuing process. With Terry's help, Evelyn is entering the community of the dead, the Kingdom of Ends, the white earth.[1]

The reference to the Spielberg film, "Back to the Future," is important. In this film, a teenage boy, triangulated in the marriage of his weak, ineffectual father and alcoholic mother, builds a car that takes him back to the time when his parents met one another. As the story unfolds, the protagonist finds that he has upstaged his father as a suitor for his mother. The girl has fallen in love with him, her future son, instead. Not only must our hero resist the temptation to commit incest with this girl whom he knows to be his mother, he must also take care not to interrupt the union of his mother and the bumbling boy who is his father. Coming between his parents (*coitus interruptus*), he realizes, would be disastrous. It would erase his very existence. Finally, after many turns and complications, the protagonist manages to get out of the middle and unite his parents. When he returns to present time he finds that his family life has changed. His father is dynamic and successful; his mother sophisticated and beautiful. During his time with them in the past he was able to subtly influence them in a positive fashion, redeeming the present. The Oedipus-complex is resolved through science fiction.

To say that the mourning process is normal, but not natural is to say that it is post-coital. The mourning process is the time-machine that takes us out of our Oedipal attachments, "back to the future." Like the protagonist in the film, we free the soul from its determinate fate by participating with it imaginally.

[1] For a thorough discussion of the *albedo* phase of alchemy and of the "white earth" see two papers by James Hillman [7].

DREAM FOUR

> I am at Evelyn's. She is excited to see me as are her children. I feel excited too, and wish to get close to her. While I'm waiting for her to get ready I go out to a nearby stream and fish. As soon as my hook hits the water I hook or snag something. I reel in my line. I have hooked a long plastic tube that smells like the rotting placentas, testicles, and dead piglets I once smelled in a pail on a hog farm.

This dream is typical of those dreams that come up from time to time as if to thwart the mourner's urge to connect back with the love-object which has been renounced. Although the Evelyn-figure, as we have seen in the previous dream, had begun to differentiate herself out from her objective correlatives, both inner (the introject) and outer (the actual woman, Evelyn), it is still common for the dream-ego to visit the place of the dreamer's old delight. Often, this sort of dream seems to be triggered by a nostalgic memory or an anniversary reaction. Indeed, the dreamer dreamt this dream on Christmas day after hearing a piece of music performed that Evelyn used to sing. The music took him back in reverie, but the dream would not indulge him. His longing, the dream suggests, is the longing for an umbilical bonding. The "long plastic tube" which he retrieves, however, is cut and has a repulsive smell "like the rotting placentas, testicles and dead piglets" he once smelled on a hog farm. The sounds which would seduce him back into the old relationship are thwarted by the stench of the incest taboo.

DREAM FIVE

> I am at Evelyn's, delighting to see her again. The house feels like home. It is spacious, rambling and bright. A slope in the floor propels me toward her and I slide backwards. I want to make love to her and I think she does to me. She seems a body of focussed passion. But this does not happen. Diane, her daughter, is home. And there are others there as well. I want to photograph her. (A few days ago a friend mentioned to me that he had a photograph of her.) The scene changes before I can get a picture. We are in the attic bedroom, a place where we have made love in the past. The room is different now. Apparently, it is an art studio. Beyond the bed on the other side of the room is a large model ship which Evelyn is making. It is as tall as I am and long too. It is a wooden sailing ship,

> complicated and grand. Evelyn tells me that she and Joni [Mitchell] have been making it. Apparently, Joni lives with her. I add that, "Yes, Joni has the know-how." I touch the boat and it slips in its stand and falls over a bit. Since it is still being constructed it is flimsy and could easily break. I right it again and keep my hands off. It is a most beautiful and impressive ship. Waking up I realize that Eveyln and Joni are building the "Ship of Death" which D. H. Lawrence wrote about. I don't need to visit Evelyn and disturb them.

Once again, the dream begins with the dream-ego returning to his old relationship as if to a scene of delight. He feels at home again. He wants to make love to Evelyn and sees her as a "body of focussed passion." His regressive, backsliding wish, however, is not fulfilled. Although, Evelyn certainly is a "body of focussed passion" her passion is no longer focussed on him. *He* may be stuck back in the old photography, wanting to take another shot for old times' sake, but *she* is not. This Evelyn is not the Evelyn of memory whom he confuses her with. She is not the Evelyn he remembers as he encounters the things in the world which remind him of that outer woman. The dream-Evelyn is discontinous with these figures. Up in the attic-bedroom where the dreamer had proviously made love to Evelyn, the dream Evelyn is constructing a beautiful model. With the help of a singer, Joni Mitchell—who the dreamer realizes "has the know-how"[2]—she is building the "Ship of Death," that "little ark" which Lawrence says must be built to take the soul through that "long and painful death/That lies between the old self and the new" [6, p. 2512].

When the dream-ego touches the ship, it shifts in its stand. He realizes that it is fragile and that he must keep his hands off. The dream-Evelyn is immersed in a creative process which he must not disturb with the assumptions, sentimentalisms and delusions of the past.

[2] The dreamer admired Joni Mitchell and listened to her as an adolescent. A stanza from her song "Cactus Tree" came to mind in connection with this dream: "There's a man who's been out sailing/ In a decade full of dreams/ And he takes her to a schooner/ And he treats her like a queen/ Bearing beads from California/ With their amber stones and green/ He has called her from the harbor/ He has kissed her with his freedom/ He has heard her off the starboard/ In the breaking and the breathing/ Of the water weeds/ While she's so busy being free."

STELLAR FRIENDS

Although these five dreams are merely the first dreams in a series of over one hundred, they bear clear witness to the imaginal background of the mourning process. As the series continues, the dream-Evelyn becomes increasingly differentiated from both the outer woman (as misperceived by the dreamer) and the introject. Though she continues to appear in dreams, and perhaps may always appear from time to time, *her appearance is no longer a function of their former relationship*. Mourning unties the specific relationship which has been rendered impossible; it does not eradicate the figure itself. On the contrary, it releases this figure from the dead relationship with which the mourner has become identified and re-connects him to the figure in an imaginal relationship. Mourning is not about getting rid of "lost objects"—despite the fact that it is always experienced as a letting go. In a deeper sense, mourning is a process by means of which the people we have objectified during our time together are recognized for who they are. The imagination cannot get rid of anything. However, as Coleridge has written, it "dissolves, diffuses, dissipates in order to re-create, or where this process is rendered impossible, yet still, at all events, it struggles to idealize and to unify" [6, p. 1588]. Mourning, in other words, does not rid us of our attachments, but of our projections. Evelyn comes back, again and again *as an image*. The imagination presents itself, again and again, *as Evelyn*. But each time she comes back she comes back differently, as if to bury each time a different objectifying assumption the dreamer had about Evelyn.

At one point, further on in the dream series, Evelyn appeared in the guise of a colleague of the dreamer. This seemed to reflect the role she was playing at that time. The dreamer had become interested in the autonomy of his psychic processes and the dream-Evelyn appeared as an assistant to help him to examine his mourning process from a less egotistic standpoint. Just as the "dead bury their own dead" (Luke 9:60), so did the Evelyn-figure in these dreams assist the dreamer in burying his previous image of the outer woman.

In other dreams, the Evelyn-figure appeared in yet other roles. In one dream she appeared as one of the characters in the repertoire of an elderly actress. Though the dream-ego experienced some erotic longings for the Evelyn-character, the old actress told him that she no longer wanted to play the same role twice. Increasingly, it seems, the Evelyn-figure came to correspond more explicitly to what Jung has called the archetype of the anima. As an anima-figure, she appeared from time to time to reconnect the energies through which the dreamer had once been bound to Evelyn to the impersonal aspects of his fate which he had dimly heeded when he realized that he must forsake that relationship. At other times her presence seemed more regressive, reflecting his longing for the familiar and his fear of life. Looking back over the dream series from the vantage point of greater understanding, the dreamer realized that his sentimental belief that Evelyn was "the woman of my dreams" had been belied by the dream-figure's refusal to be that woman even in his dreams. From the autonomy of the dream-Evelyn he learned to appreciate, as he never really had while in the thick of relationship, the autonomy of the actual woman as a person in her own right with a fate of her own. The dream-Evelyn, far from being a mere introject or hyper-cathected libidinal trend, was, as are all projections once taken back and integrated, an organ of perception through which the dreamer could now see both himself and Evelyn more accurately. Such is the angelic function of projection. While it obscures the object upon which it is projected so that we see as "through a glass darkly," taken back (creatively retained) it cleanses the "doors of perception" allowing us for the first time to see each other "face to face."

Though he dreams less of Evelyn now, the dreamer realized that he and she continue to be connected, though now "beyond the mist of affects," in that subtle union which Nietzsche described as "Stellar Friendship." Let us conclude this chapter by quoting again from this passage [7, pp. 216-217]:

> That we had to become strangers to one another is the law to which we are *subject*: just by that shall we become more sacred to one another! Just by that shall the thought of our former friendship become holier! There is probably some immense, invisible curve and stellar orbit in which our courses and goals, so widely different, may be *comprehended* as small stages of the way,—let us raise ourselves to this thought! But our life is too short, and our power of vision too limited for us to be more than friends in the sense of this sublime possibility.—And so we will *believe* in our stellar friendship, though we should have to be terrestrial enemies to one another.

REFERENCES

1. J. Hillman, *Inter Views*, Harper & Row, New York, 1983.
2. C. G. Jung, *Letters, Vol. 1: 1909-1950*, R. F. C. Hull (trans.), Princeton University Press, Princeton, 1973.

3. T. S. Eliot, *Collected Poems, 1909-1962*, Faber & Faber, London, 1963.
4. S. Freud, *The Ego and the Id*, J. Rivere (trans.), W. W. Norton, New York, 1962.
5. C. G. Jung, *Symbols of Transformation, Collected Works*, Vol. 5, R. F. C. Hull (trans.), Princeton University Press, Princeton, 1967.
6. M. H. Abrams et al. (eds.), *The Norton Anthology of English Literature*, third edition, W. W. Norton, New York, 1975.
7. J. Hillman, Silver and the White Earth, Part One and Two, in *Spring: An Annual of Archetypal Psychology and Jungian Thought*, Spring Publications, Dallas, 1980-1981.
8. J. Mitchell, *Joni Mitchell*, D. Crosby (producer), Seven Arts Records.
9. F. Nietzsche, *Joyful Wisdom*, T. Common (trans.), Frederick Unger Publishing, New York, 1960.

11.17.07

CHAPTER 7

What Do the Dead Want?

This living hand, now warm and capable
Of earnest grasping, would, if it were cold
And in the icy silence of the tomb,
So haunt thy days and chill thy dreaming nights
That thou wouldst wish thine own heart dry of blood
So in my veins red life might stream again,
And thou be conscience-calm'd—see here it is—
I hold it towards you [1, p. 1205].

John Keats

FROM PROCESS TO MYSTERY

The life sciences look for commonalities across large samples, repeatable results, causal relationships, generalities. When the grief of the bereaved is approached in this manner a mourning process comprised of a number of stages can be described. While this kind of knowledge helps the bereaved to embrace their grief as a normal part of bereavement, the actual work of mourning is a matter as individual as the loss itself. Even if our dear ones died together in a car accident, or still more collectively, in a battle or a concentration camp, we cannot properly mourn them in such mass graves. Each person is from a sample of one, and it is only by distinguishing his or her irreplicable uniqueness that the work of mourning can proceed. The most important variable of the mourning process, regardless of the "stage" the bereaved appear to be in, is the identity of the deceased. Though a widow may seem to have more in common with another widow than with someone experiencing another sort of loss, in a deeper sense, each woman's process is as different as were the men they called their husbands. Ann's bereavement differs from Mary's, not merely because they are different, but because their husbands, Jack and George were/are different. Though comparisons can be drawn across a sample of mourners (parents, widows, widowers etc.), the inner world of mourning is as unique as the fingerprints of the deceased. In the final analysis, the vicissitudes of our grief and mourning are a function of the loved ones we have lost. Their personalities are an even more important factor than our own. The fact that Jack was an embittered alcoholic and the fact that George was a man who lived a full and creative life are major determinants of the mourning process of those who survive them. The dead themselves supply the metaphors upon which the mourning process of the bereaved is modelled. Some people are more difficult to mourn than others. Getting to know the dead, helping them complete their soul-making, and understanding them from the point of view death brings is what mourning is all about. The process, despite what we know about it from the "outside" and in general, is, when considered from the "inside" and on a case-by-case basis, a mystery. Despite the fact that our loved ones are "gone," they still influence us, each in their own inimitable style. In symptoms, dreams, and moods they return. What do they want from us? What do they need?

UNFINISHED BUSINESS

When their loved ones pass away, the bereaved may feel burdened by what they failed to express to them. In reproaching themselves for love that was not told, complaints that were petty, pride that would not make amends, and appreciation felt too late, the bereaved express the bitterness of their loss. These sentiments, however, are not the exclusive property of the living. The dead may also have "unfinished business." Indeed, their regrets may be mixed up with ours. In bereavement the boundaries between the living and the dead are not clear. Seeing themselves as the only persons left for emotions and ideas to belong to, the bereaved tend to identify with the emotions and ideas which animate their bereavement, even though many of these ideas are underpinned by the images of the dead. But is it we who are ruminating about them, or they who are ruminating about us? Is it only our regrets we feel or is it also theirs? Whatever the answer, one thing is certain: we could not mourn without them. Present in their absence, the dead are the material, formal, and final causes of the bereavement mystery.

Nothing weighs so heavily upon a mourner's heart than the passing of a life that has been unsatisfactorily or incompletely lived. And yet, most of us will die such deaths. The reaper's scythe cuts a random, arbitrary swath. The thread of a loved one's life is severed by tumor and disease, accident and suicide more often than by the ripeness of completion—or so, at least, it seems to the bereaved. Children in the flower of their youth, adolescents by their own hand, the elderly before their wisdom has been shared, anyone at any time by cancer: the more truncated the lives of the deceased the more difficult they are to grieve. The necessity of mourning is largely a function of the arbitrariness of death itself. Often it is the sheer senselessness of a dear one's death that initiates a depressive search for meaning on the part of the bereaved.

David Eddy, a strategic family therapist, recently published the case study of a young boy who began to experience suicidal ideas as the anniversary date of his elder brother's suicide approached [2, pp. 32-33]. The intervention which helped the boy and his family required that they each anonymously do things in the spirit of the dead brother, things that would finish the dead boy's dreams and more fully define the wholeness of even such an incomplete life. On an annual basis the family were directed to honor the deceased brother by meeting together and planning a good deed which they would do as a family on his behalf. Though this case was written up to describe the power and range of strategic therapy, it demonstrates, as well, something of the imaginal background of the mourning process. Jung's comment, "I frequently have a feeling that [the dead] are standing directly behind us, waiting to hear what answer we will give to them, and what answer to destiny" [3, p. 308], must somehow have been the haunting experience of this boy's bereavement as well. Indeed, his suicidal ideas can be imagined to be not his at all but, rather, a legacy passed on from his brother. But what answer does a little boy make to an elder brother who has despaired of his life? Not easy by any means. Far more likely to fall prey to the same despair.[1] By restoring the dialectical

[1] The serial suicides that we occasionally meet among adolescents may be imagined against this background. The bereaved survivors, unable to work through the despair of their friends, identify with it and become suicidal themselves.

relationship between the living and the dead, however, therapy helped this suicidal boy to differentiate out from his identification with his dead brother while at the same time restoring the dead brother to the family as a spiritual reality. Through their attempts to finish the dead boy's dreams the family members could each make answer to the questions, frustrations, and despair which the elder brother was unable to resolve during his own life.

Sometimes the bereaved, having misread the lives of those they grieve, have corrective experiences which give them solace. The mourning process of a middle-aged woman whose father died in advanced old age was complicated by her concerns about his state in the afterlife. Insecure about his love for her, she tended to view him as a hard man, and worried that his character flaws would keep him out of the Kingdom. After several weeks of worrying over this, she had a vision of her father. He stood at the foot of her bed for a few moments, in the body he had as a young man of twenty-five, and smiled at her reassuringly. This vision afforded the woman a new view of her father, a view which unblocked her mourning. It was not so much that the vision fulfilled her wish to be loved. Deeper than that, it freed her from her critical view of his life and allowed her to imagine into the wholeness of who he more objectively was. Like the father who is able to protect his child from its own aggressive impulses by remaining strong in the face of the hostility that the child occasionally expressed toward him, the father in this vision appears with a robustness that assures his daughter that he does not reside in the hell to which she had assigned him. The worries of the daughter vanished. Her father *had* taken care of his business. Less was left over for her than she had at first believed. Indeed, it was mostly her own projections that she had found oppressive, and even these her father lovingly returned by revealing himself to her in the angelic body of his ongoing imaginal life, or as Blake would say, in "the lineaments of gratified desire" [4, p. 63].

In his autobiography, Jung, too, tells a story about a crucial loss, the mourning of which was facilitated by the image of the lost loved one. Shortly after his wife died, Jung awoke from a dream with the feeling that he had spent a whole day with her in the south of France where she was continuing the work on the Grail legend that she had left unfinished at her death. Commenting on the experience Jung writes: "The thought that my wife was continuing after death to work on her further spiritual development—however that may be conceived—struck me as meaningful and held a measure of reassurance for me"

[3, p. 309]. Again, as in the previous example, the realization that the deceased has not left as much unfinished business behind as had at first been thought, and even continues to work on the bit that was left unfinished, consoles the bereaved husband, Jung. Despite her importance in his life, he will not have to mourn her as laboriously as he did others who lived less completed lives.[2]

JUNG AND THE "HEREAFTER"

> It is important and salutary to speak also of incomprehensible things . . . [3, p. 300].

Jung's dream of spending the day with his late wife in the south of France is but one of many experiences he had relating to the question of the "life" of the dead, or life after death. In themselves, these experiences are not particularly uncommon. Many who have experienced bereavement or have worked clinically with the bereaved report similar experiences. Jung's *thoughts* about these experiences, however, are of considerable interest. Though he is meticulously precise in conveying to his readers his awareness of the impossibility, on epistemological grounds, of ever making knowledge claims about the question of life after death, he also stresses the importance of "mythologizing" about the subject. In Jung's view, our ideas about the dead and the hereafter must be given attentive consideration despite our rationalistic prejudice against doing so for the simple reason that they are the spontaneous contents of our psychic inventory. As Jung puts it [3, pp. 299-300]:

> It is not that I wish we had a life after death. In fact, I would prefer not to foster such ideas. Still, I must state, to give reality its due, that, without my wishing and without my doing anything about it, thoughts of this nature move about within me. I can't say whether these thoughts are true or false, but I do know they are there, and can be given utterance, if I do not repress them out of some prejudice. Prejudice cripples and injures the full phenomenon

[2] Jung's mourning of his wife was facilitated by creative work. As he put it in his autobiography: "Everything that I have written this year and last year, 'The Undiscovered Self,' 'Flying Saucers: A Modern Myth,' 'A psychological View of Conscience,' has grown out of the stone sculptures I did after my wife's death" [3, p. 175].

> of psychic life. And I know too little about psychic life to feel that I can set it right out of superior knowledge.

As a phenomenologist of the psyche, Jung could not dismiss the experiences of the bereaved, the dreams and visions which pertain to death, or the mythological and religious ideas about life after death. Nor could he, in the manner of Freud, explain these phenomena away by reducing them to known psychodynamic processes. Psychic phenomena that lie outside the reach of scientific inquiry must be saved, in Jung's view, from dismissive rationalism on the one hand, and wooly-minded credulity on the other. In place of these two attitudes, Jung suggests another, more data-friendly position [3, p. 302].

> If there is something we cannot know, we must necessarily abandon it as an intellectual problem. For example, I do not know for what reason the universe came into being, and shall never know. Therefore I must drop this question as a scientific or intellectual problem. But if an idea about it is offered to me—in dreams or in mythic traditions—I ought to take note of it. I even ought to build up a conception on the basis of such hints, even though it will forever remain a hypothesis which I know cannot be proved.

Though it is important to recognize and respect the limits of science, it is also important not to split oneself off from the experiences one has which fall outside those limits. One can be a rigorous scientist as well as a religious or spiritual person. Indeed, if we are to live our wholeness and not repress the "facts" of our experience, both attitudes are essential. Our extra-scientific and other-worldly experiences and concerns are as intrinsic to our lives and fate as are our this-worldly and scientific ones. We must give both their due, each in the manner dictated by the phenomenon at hand. While in the one case we may achieve *knowledge* we can live by, in the other we may create a *fiction* or *mythology* which will help us to live that aspect of our nature which is mysterious to us. Although much of what we are we shall never know or be able to demonstrate scientifically, it is still important to inhabit ourselves as fully as possible [3, p. 302].

> Reason sets the boundaries far too narrowly for us, and would have us accept only the known—and that too with limitations—and live in a known framework, just as if we were sure how far life actually extends. As a matter of fact, day after day we live far

> beyond the bounds of our consciousness; without our knowledge, the life of the unconscious is going on within us. The more the critical reason dominates, the more impoverished life becomes; but the more the unconscious, and the more myth we are capable of making conscious, the more of life we integrate.

What is unique and individual about each of us and each of our lost loved ones extends beyond the bounds of scientific comprehension. Though we can each participate as subjects in well-designed research studies, the commonalities that emerge after the statistical analysis has been completed bear little resemblance to who we uniquely are. The individual is not the object of science, and yet it is precisely this mystery of individuality that we must live in ourselves and mourn in others.

METHOD OF NECESSARY STATEMENT

Having rehearsed Jung's position regarding the importance of speculating about "incomprehensible things," especially the problem of death and the "hereafter," let us now examine some of his ideas about methodology. Since the issue cannot be approached as an intellectual problem, Jung suggests that we build a "mythology" of death by taking into account the data which can be gleaned from dreams, visions, mythic traditions and parapsychology. What does the psyche say about the hereafter? What are the dead doing in the dreams of the bereaved or in the dreams of those anticipating death? What is it that they want? To "mythologize" a tentative, yet livable, answer to the question of life after death, Jung recommends a procedure which he calls "the method of necessary statement" [3, p. 310]. This method "represents the principle of *amplification* in the interpretation of dreams" [3, p. 310]. The imagination, in Jung's view, is limited by the images it is imagining about. What we say about a figure of fantasy is not arbitrary but governed by that figure. The number one, Jung notes by way of example, "as the first numeral, is unity . . . but it is also '*the unity*', the One, All-Oneness, individuality and non-duality—not a numeral but a philosophical concept, an archetype and attribute of God, the monad" [3, p. 310]. Other numerals would necessitate quite other statements. These particular statements, however, are "governed by the nature of oneness" [3, p. 310]. Though Jung could have chosen other ways to demonstrate the method of necessary statement and the principle of amplification (color, for example), he writes of simple whole numbers in this context because mathematics has further heuristic value for a speculative psychology. Like the pure mathematician working out the equations for relationships which go beyond the pale of empirical understanding (only later to discover that they have actually anticipated the behavior of matter), Jung suggests it is important to practice a pure psychology, that is, to permit the "disciplined imagination to build up images of intangibles by logical principles and on the basis of empirical data, that is, on the evidence of dreams" [3, p. 310]. On the analogy with mathematics, Jung suggests that if we allow ourselves to entertain "incomprehensible things" with a "disciplined imagination," we may be rewarded at some later date with more complete knowledge of the processes these images point to [3, p. 311].

> I submit that other than mathematical statements (i.e., statements implicit in nature) are likewise capable of pointing to irrepresentable realities beyond themselves—such, for example, as those products of the imagination which enjoy universal acceptance or are distinguished by the frequency of their occurrence, like the whole class of archetypal motifs. Just as in the case of some factors in mathematical equations we cannot say to what physical realities they correspond, so in the case of some mythological products we do not know at first to what psychic realities they refer. Equations governing the turbulence of heated gases existed long before the problems of such gases had been precisely investigated. Similarly, we have long been in possession of mythologems which express the dynamics of certain subliminal processes, though these processes were only given names in very recent times.

JUNG'S MYTHOLOGY

Jung's mythology of the dead, a mythology informed by his own dreams as well as those of his patients, hypothesizes that life continues after death in an imaginal form. This hypothesis Jung based on two types of experiences. In the first place, he was impressed by the fact that the unconscious does not anticipate or imagine the end of bodily life as a final end. The terminally ill, as anyone working with the dying can easily ascertain, typically dream that another sort of life awaits them on the other side of that river which divides the living from the dead, a life which may or may not correspond with their previous images of an afterlife or with their wishes for one. In the second place, Jung was impressed by those dreams and visions of the *bereaved* which also suggest that the dead continue to live on in some manner. Though it is tempting to rationalize away these experiences, some of them are so uncanny that they almost seem intended to counteract this tendency. Jung, for instance, tells of lying awake in bed the day after the funeral of a neighbor who had been his friend. While thinking about his late friend, Jung had a vivid impression that this man was standing at the foot of his bed. At first Jung told himself that the figure was merely a spurious fantasy. Like Chuangtzu pondering the question of whether he was a man who had just dreamed he was a butterfly or a butterfly now dreaming he was a man, however, Jung reminded himself that he had no proof that the apparition was merely illusory. Suspending his disbelief, he decided to interact with the image of his late friend as if it had an objective reality. The figure beckoned Jung to follow him, and in imagination the two walked next door to where the friend had lived. Once inside, they went into the study whereupon the friend walked over to a bookshelf and pointed to "the second of five books with red bindings which stood on the second shelf from the top" [3, p. 312]. Here the vision ended. Jung was not acquainted with his friend's library and found it peculiar that a particular book should be emphasized. The next morning he asked his friend's widow to let him into her husband's library. Just as in his vision, Jung found the five red books on the second shelf from the top. They were a collection of novels by Emile Zola. Jung was struck by the title of the second volume, the book indicated in his vision. The book was titled: "The Legacy of the Dead."

EDUCATING THE DEAD

Perhaps the most interesting idea which Jung shares with us on the subject of life after death is the notion that the dead are vitally interested in the knowledge of the living. Among the experiences upon which this view is based was that of one of Jung's pupils, a woman in her sixties, who had a dream about the dead which seemed to compensate for her reluctance to begin thinking about her own mortality. In her dream, the woman found herself in the hereafter. A class was going on. Among the pupils who were assembled she noticed various deceased friends. She looked around for a teacher, but didn't see anyone playing that role. At last she realized that it was she who was to teach them.

Apparently, after death the dead wish to learn from the newly deceased about more contemporary life experiences, "just as if the acts and experiences taking place in earthly life, in time and space, were the decisive ones" [3, p. 305].

Another experience, this time Jung's, suggests that the dead turn to the living with the hope of learning from them. Several months before his mother's sudden and unexpected death, Jung met the shade of his long-dead father in a dream. Although he would very much have liked to tell his father about himself, his family, and his professional accomplishments, he sensed that his father had another agenda. And, indeed, that turned out to be the case. The elder Jung asked his son to teach him what he, as a psychologist, knew of marital psychology. Commenting on this dream, Jung suggests that the dream presaged his mother's death. His parents, not unlike many couples, had had a difficult marriage, and Jung concludes that his father was interested in learning more about marriage since he would soon be resuming his marital relationship [3, pp. 315-316].

> Evidently he had acquired no better understanding in his timeless state and therefore had to appeal to someone among the living who, enjoying the benefits of changed times, might have a fresh approach to the whole thing.

Jung, it should be noted, did answer the question his father put to him. Following his mother's death in January 1923, he wrote a paper, "Marriage as a Psychological Relationship" (1925).

Recently, a relative of my own, who had been diagnosed with a terminal cancer, told me a dream which once again contains the suggestion that the dead wish to learn things from the newly deceased. In his dream, the dreamer is to drive his small car, a car which he referred to humorously as his "mighty Escort,"[3] through the waters of the South Saskatchewan river to the other side where he was to give lectures in various town halls. When he saw the other cars at the river bank with their huge tires and four-wheel drive transmissions, he became doubtful of his own car's ability to make the crossing. Before attempting the passage he decided to take his car to a local garage to have it checked over by mechanics. In the context of the medical

[3] He drove a Ford Escort

diagnosis which had preceded the dream, the river can be understood as that archetypal river that divides the here from the hereafter.[4] Saskatchewan was his place of origin and it is entirely fitting that it is the South Saskatchewan river which he must cross to find his entrance into death. Though the doctors told him just prior to the dream that he would live for only a very short time, the dream suggests that actually there will be a delay. He is not sure that his car can make it across. At the brink of death, he realizes that he requires repair before he can attempt the passage. *Death can be put off for a while until he has prepared himself for it with further soul-making,* (As I write these lines, a year and a half has passed since the diagnosis was made and the dreamer has remained in fairly good health despite some advance in the disease.) As in the previous examples, there is in this dream a reference to teaching. The dreamer is scheduled to deliver lectures to the ancestor spirits who live on the "other side" of the place where he was born.

Drawing conclusions from a large number of experiences such as these, Jung writes [3, p. 308]:

> People have the idea that the dead know far more than we, for Christian doctrine teaches that in the hereafter we shall "see face to face." Apparently, however, the souls of the dead "know" only what they knew at the moment of death, and nothing beyond that. Hence their endeavor to penetrate into life in order to share in the knowledge of men. . . . It seems to me as if they were dependent on the living for receiving answers to their questions, that is, on those who have survived them and exist in a world of change: as if omniscience or, as I might put it, omniconsciousness, were not at their disposal, but could flow only into the psyche of the living, into a soul bound to a body. The mind of the living appears, therefore, to hold an advantage over that of the dead in at least one point: in the capacity for attaining clear and decisive cognitions.

The clarity of cognition, in Jung's view, is a function of the oppositions of the *incarnational* world.[5] It requires spatial and temporal distinctions, distinctions which are assumed to no longer hold sway in

[4] For a thorough account of the river as the boundary between the world of the living and the realm of the dead see a work by Holger Kalweit [5].

[5] "Cognition, like generation, presupposes an opposition, a here and there, an above and below, a before and after" [3, p. 308].

eternity: male and female, good and evil, above and below, before and after, to be or not to be. Though these qualities continue to "exist" in the beyond, there they lack the distinctiveness—and hence the effectiveness for individuation—which characterizes their manifestation in the four-dimensional world of space-time.[6] Though death is frequently imagined as a state free from the conflicts of life, it would be an error to assume that death actually resolves these conflicts. The "diffuse omniscience" or "subjectless consciousness" [3, p. 308] of the hereafter tends to blur the distinction between the opposites, making it impossible for the dead to struggle with them as the living do. At death the process of individuation is arrested. To the extent that the dead were unable to individuate in life, they become dissolved into the collective unconscious. It is in this sense that they are "unredeemed." Since the ultimate goal of the soul is perfect wholeness through individuation, the dead must continue to work on their spiritual development [3, p. 309]. Yet, in their state of dissolution, they are unable to do so.

It is precisely for this reason that the living have a part to play in the "redemption" of the dead. The animating blood[7] of our animal souls—imagination, the blood of the psyche—breathes "life" into the dead, drawing them back from Limbo and into

[6] In the "Seven Sermons to the Dead," a piece of active imagination in the style of a Gnostic creation myth, Jung addresses the soul of the dead Christians who did not find what they wanted in Jerusalem and teaches them, among other things, about the opposites. He speaks of two orders of Being, pleroma and creatura. In the pleroma, qualities are paired with their opposites in a manner which renders them balanced and void. The pleroma is an eternal world which is not confined by the categories of time and space. In the realm of creatura, on the other hand, the "pleroma is rent in us" [3, p. 381], and we incarnate its "qualities in the name and sign of distinctiveness." Jung explains to his audience that we must keep to our nature, which is distinctiveness, by differentiating ourselves from qualities and, thereby, their opposites. This is the "PRINCIPIUM INDIVIDUATIONIS" [3, p. 380], the individuation process. The danger of not individuating, not distinguishing ourselves from those qualities which would make us all the same, is that "we fall into the pleroma itself and cease to be creatures" [3, p. 380]. This, presumably, is what happens at death. Whatever we have failed to make distinct and conscious in ourselves, "falleth into the pleroma [where it] is made void by its opposite" [3, p. 382]. The dead, who have fallen into the pleroma become, as it were, our "karma." It then falls to us to take up the problem of *their* individuation, if only to differentiate from it in our own lives.

[7] In the Homeric underworld, the dead are forlorn, indefinite images who require offerings of living blood in order to assume, momentarily, the definiteness necessary to speak.

our dreams and visions.[8] Like Odysseus journeying through the Underworld, we journey through "death's dream kingdom," teaching and learning as we go. We offer the dead the fruits of our struggle with the opposites in the ongoing process of the evolution of consciousness, and in empathizing with them in the pain of their unresolved conflicts we gain insights into the direction and meaning of our own lives.

When we ourselves die, we continue this work of redemption. As Christ, when he died, "descended into Hell" [7, p. 377] (that is, *Gehenna*, the Hebrew Underworld, the world of the dead) and preached the "gospel" of victory in his struggle with the opposites to the "spirits in prison" (1 Peter 3: 19) so that they "though judged in the flesh like men, . . . might live in the spirit like God" (1 Peter 4: 6), so we, as we enter the grave, bring answers[9] that we have worked out in our own lives to the questions posed by the lives of those who have gone before us.

Then, as we are accepted into the community of the dead [9, p. 185], we wait for our own redemption as future generations seek to find answers to the questions that our lives have raised [3, pp. 308-309].

> If there were to be a conscious existence after death, it would, so it seems to me, have to continue on the level of consciousness attained by humanity, which in any age has an upper though variable limit. There are many beings who throughout their lives and at the moment of death lag behind their own potentialities and—even more important—behind the knowledge which has been brought to consciousness by other human beings during their own

[8] The sacrifice of blood which allows the dead to manifest themselves might also be understood as an *abaissement du niveau mental* (Janet), a lowering of the mental level. As Jung, who frequently made use of this notion, wrote in a preface to a book approaching the subject of death dreams and ghosts from the psychological angle: "An integral component of any nocturnal, numinous experience is a dimming of [our] consciousness, the feeling that one is in the grip of something greater than oneself, the impossibility of exercising criticism [at the time], and the paralysis of the will" [6, p. vii].

[9] "[A]mong the Ainus [of Japan], we are told, when a funeral ceremony is performed, the master of the family becomes the celebrant. 'You are a god now,' he says to the corpse, 'And without hankering after this world, you are to go now to the world of the gods, where your ancestors abide. *They will thank you for the presents that you bring* . . . (italics mine) [8, p. 343].

lifetimes. Hence their demand to attain in death that share of awareness which they failed to attain in their own lifetimes.

JUNG'S DIALOGUE WITH THE DEAD

Although he never explicitly wrote about life after death in his professional writings, in his autobiography Jung states that the subtext of his entire life's work has been "the question of the interplay between the 'here' and the 'hereafter' [3, p. 299]. Throughout his life Jung was haunted by the questions of the dead and felt called to make his answer to them. His pastor father's empty spiritual life, not to mention his uncanny experience of the dead who came "back from Jerusalem where they found not what they sought" [3, p. 191], led him to turn his psychotherapeutic interest to the problem of Christian psychology [3, pp. 191-192].

> The dead have become ever more distinct for me as the voices of the Unanswered, Unresolved, and Unredeemed; for since the questions and demands which my destiny required me to answer did not come to me from outside, they must have come from the inner world. These conversations with the dead formed a kind of prelude to what I had to communicate to the world about the unconscious: a kind of pattern of order and interpretation of its general contents.

Nietzsche's failure to live the Dionysian compensation to Christianity which he had preached and Goethe's failure to find solutions to the problems raised in his *Faust* posed yet other questions for him. And then there was "the restless Wotan-Hermes of my Alemannic and Frankish ancestors who poses challenging riddles—the whole German problem" [3, p. 318].

THE WISDOM OF THE DEAD

Though the dead may wish to share in the knowledge of the living in the manner described by Jung, the living also call upon the wisdom of the dead. In 1 Samuel, for example, we read that Saul, cut off from God and intimidated by the Philistines, consulted the dead Samuel through the medium of Endor and sought his guidance (1 Samuel 28: 7-20). Likewise, in book eleven of the Odyssey, Odysseus, as we mentioned above, journeys to "the House of Hades and of dread Persephone" to find out from the ghost of the prophet Teiresias how to get home to Ithica. More recently, New Age adherents turn increasingly to the dead for counsel and direction. Troubled "believers" regularly consult the disembodied spirits of such notables as Elvis, Tutankhamen, and Marilyn Monroe through "channellers"—not the least of which is Shirley MacLaine.

The Bible takes a dim view of such practices. In Leviticus, for instance, the Lord specifically commands his people not to turn to mediums and spiritists (Lev. 19: 31). And in Isaiah the practice is again contrasted negatively with allegiance to the Lord: "And when they say to you, 'Consult the mediums and the spiritists who whisper and mutter,' should not a people consult their God? Should they consult the dead on behalf of the living?" (Isaiah 8: 19). The concern seems to be that the Israelites will break ranks and worship other spirits before God. Indeed, in Deuteronomy this is the concern about dreams. By order of law "a prophet or a dreamer of dreams" was to be recognized as false and put to death if he spoke to the people saying, "'Let us go after other gods (whom you have not known) and let us serve them'" (Deut. 13: 1-5).

Doubtless, one must be cautious in approaching this whole area. Granting undue authority to the voices of the unconscious might lead suggestible minds into delusion. This does not mean, however, that we must turn away from the dead altogether—only that we should greet them with our critical capacities intact. To turn away from the dead would be to turn away from culture itself. We consult the dead whenever we walk into a library, or open a book. The Bible is a case in point. Everyone in it is dead and yet it is the Living Word to which believers regularly turn for counsel. Even the people in the Bible look back to their forebears. The student poring over Plato and Aristotle, Dickens and Proust is also listening to the voices of the dead, and, if he writes a paper on them, is in conversation with them as well. Sometimes it is they who teach us and sometimes it is we who teach them. Though Blake learned much from his predecessor Milton, he also had things to teach him. Recognizing the extent to which the dead Milton was locked up in *Paradise Lost*, Puritanism, and his wives and daughters, Blake wrote his great poem *Milton* in order to release him [10].

Culture is erotic. As in Plato's *Symposium*, all the spirits are invited to rap around the table. The psychology of the living is underpinned by the dead. Their ideas, opinions, attitudes, emotions, acts, deeds and questions move through our souls even as we move through theirs.

Love and death are ahistorical. They embrace in anachronism, dovetail in the Now. We don't need to attend a seance. We are our own medium. The dead are as near at hand as the vague, pervasive feelings which haunt our lives. By day we see them through a glass darkly, but in our dreams we see them face to face.

"We can never know what to want," writes Milan Kundera in *The Unbearable Lightness of Being*, "because living only one life, we can neither compare it with our previous lives nor perfect it in our lives to come" [11, p. 8]. The remedy for the free-floating anxiety which makes our lives so unbearably light and directionless is an awareness of the lives that have gone before us into the grave. The souls of the dead lend weight to our own. Indeed, without death there would be no gravity in the psyche, no meaning in our lives. Even our orientation in time and space is a function of the liberation the dead have obtained from these categories. Coming back from the light after a near-death experience, or from the funeral of a dear one, we discover time and space in a different aspect. They lose their hold on us as we continue to hold on to the dead. In the immediacy of death love travels faster than light, and time and space become relative. No longer relevant to the dead, these dimensions are no longer quite so absolute for us either. The same could be said of the polarities we experience in space-time: up and down, in and out, backwards and forwards, male and female, good and evil, pain and pleasure, etc. Our love ceases to be entirely subject to these oppositions to the extent that it is directed towards the dead, who no longer exist within them. Though we continue to live the opposites, perspectives beyond them—the perspectives of the dead—inform our movements through them. As we help the dead to inhabit death; they help us to inhabit life. We are as much their angels as they are ours. "As we grow older," writes Eliot in *Four Quartets* [12, p. 203],

> The world becomes stranger, the pattern more complicated
> Of dead and living. Not the intense moment
> Isolated, with no before and after,
> But a lifetime burning in every moment
> And not the lifetime of one man only
> But of old stones that cannot be deciphered.
> There is a time for the evening under starlight,
> A time for the evening under lamplight
> (The evening with the photograph album).
> Love is most nearly itself
> When here and now cease to matter. . . .

MOURNING AND THE IRRATIONAL

I wept, and nothing happened, and you did not come.

[cited in 13, p. 309]
Sarah Ferguson

There is a rational aspect to the mourning process: reality-testing and decathexis, letting go and saying good-bye. But there is also an irrational aspect: mourning has to do with the greeting of angels. These two aspects of the process, the rational farewell and the mystical hello, may enact themselves concurrently or sequentially. In some cases, a loss may seem to have been satisfactorily grieved with little or no reference made to the fate of the dead until they return, years later, in a dream or a therapy hour. In other cases, the bereaved are simply unable to let go of the dead until they are greeted by them again as angels. The relationship between these two modes of mourning may be similar to what St. Augustine meant when he suggested that it is only the hand that has become open by letting go of what it had held that can properly receive. We must add, however, that for some the opposite of this is true as well: only by realizing that we are clinging to an angel can we relax the grip on our dear one.

In this rational age the irrational part of the mourning process may pose special problems. Indeed, some grievers may find it difficult to access this aspect of the process, especially if they have grown up bereft of a religious or spiritual framework. The psychotherapist today regularly finds himself working with people who, unable to imagine the autonomy of their dead friends and relatives, have rendered themselves living parodies of them.[10]

FIELD OF DREAMS

Art is a house that tries to be haunted.

Emily Dickinson

[10]I am thinking of the husband who leaves his wife and moves in with his mother after his father dies, and of the little girl who is fearful of the onset of puberty because this would be to grow away from her resemblance to a best friend who recently died. Also to be included here is the man who is described by his spouse as having "become a zombie" after his parents died ten years ago.

A recent American film, "Field of Dreams" [14], starring Kevin Costner depicts the irrational aspect of the mourning process in a masterful fashion. Costner plays the role of a thirty-six year old, university educated man who has moved with his wife and daughter to Iowa to try his hand at farming. As the story unfolds, we learn that he was raised by his father, but had a falling-out with him as a teenager and left home on a bad note. The fight was ostensibly about baseball. The father and son had been passionately interested in the game and the son, in a moment of gratuitous rebellion, had maligned one of his father's baseball heroes, "Shoeless" Joe Jackson, a great hitter who had been dismissed from the League after being wrongfully implicated in a scandal. The father died without the son ever making contact with him again and the son felt regret for his behavior toward his father.

One day, while walking through a tall crop of corn on his farm, the Costner-character hears a voice. It is clearly an uncanny, unfamiliar experience. At first he does not believe his ears and reaches for rational explanations for it. None can be found. Later that night he is awakened from his sleep by the same voice. Its message is the same as before: "If you build it, he will come."

For some time, the farmer, Costner, broods upon the meaning of this sentence. Once more he hears it imploring him in the cornfield. This time, however, it is accompanied by a vision. He sees, in the middle of his field, a baseball diamond, fully lighted up with flood-lights. He realizes with an inner certainty that it is a baseball diamond that he must build. Somehow he knows that if he builds such a diamond, "Shoeless" Joe Jackson, his father's hero, will return from the dead and play ball once more.

The verdant farm and the happy family life are an idyllic backdrop to the Costner-character's mid-life anxieties. Although his father has long been dead and although there is no outward sign of any continued preoccupation with him, when Costner articulates his anxieties to his wife we learn that they are underpinned by his (faulty) perceptions of his father's life.

> I'm thirty-six years's old. I have a wife, a child, and a mortgage, and I'm scared to death I'm turning into my father.

In answer to his wife's query as to what his father has to do with all this, the Costner character replies:

> I never forgave him for getting old. By the time he was as old as I am now he was ancient. He must have had dreams, but he never did anything about them. For all I know he may have heard voices too, but he sure didn't listen to them. The man never did one spontaneous thing in all the years I knew him and I'm afraid of that happening to me. And something tells me this might be my last chance to do anything about it. . . .

With the support of his wife and daughter, Costner ploughs down a large section of his corn and builds a full-sized baseball diamond, complete with flood-lights and bleachers. The neighbors, of course, think he is crazy.

Day by day, he watches the diamond from the window of his house. The seasons change, winter sets in. The waiting begins to take on a mournful quality. We feel the emptiness of the receptive attitude. Has the whole thing been sheer madness? Can the farm survive with so much land taken out of production? (Is the grief pathological?) Wouldn't it make more sense to plough the whole thing under and farm the land once more? Then, on the baseball diamond, there appears a man in a white baseball uniform. It is "Shoeless" Joe Jackson—his father's idol. Costner greets him and the two play ball together. "Shoeless" Joe is grateful to play again. He compares his expulsion from baseball to an amputation, and it is clear that he is now being healed. This healing of the father's ideal foreshadows the coming of the Costner-character's father and the climax of the film.

As the story unfolds still further, the voice sends other messages, and the field becomes more populated. The characters that convene upon the field, some living, some dead, thicken the plot of each other's lives in a manner that allows each to complete what was unfinished about their lives.

This film, no less than the poem of a great elegist, teaches us how to mourn. The Costner-character models for us precisely that openness to the irrational that is necessary if we are to engage with the spirits of the dead which reside in the dead-zones of the psyche and the dead-spots in our hearts. The naive simplicity of the film's protagonist must be cultivated in the bereaved. Indeed, like the Costner-character, we may imagine that they too are being implored from the beyond to honor the imagination with further imagining. By granting reality to the voices and impulses that sound within them, the bereaved may enable the dead to individuate themselves more completely.

When Jung credited the figure of his late friend with objective reality and walked with him to his library he was befriending the mourning process. Had his been a baseball story, it would probably have been on a baseball diamond and not in the library of a scholar that he greeted the angel.

The voice in the cornfield imploring the film's protagonist to build a baseball diamond has a broader meaning. The connection it draws between *building something* and the *coming of the dead* suggests that mourning is a creative process. If we build a baseball diamond, write a novel, paint a picture, or compose a poem, the dead, whose fate is bound up with our own, will have a place to manifest themselves. Keats, in his poem, "Ode to Psyche," draws the same connection. Dedicating himself as poet to the psyche he writes [15, p. 204]:

> Yes, I will be thy priest, and build a fane
> In some untrodden region of my mind,
> Where branched thoughts, new grown with pleasant pain,
> Instead of pines shall murmur in the wind. . . .

These lines could be read as elegy without diminishing Keats's pledge to the soul. Indeed, each of us could utter them with a different dear one in mind. Whether it is by finishing the dreams of a suicidal brother or by building a baseball diamond in order to redeem the soul of "Shoeless" Joe Jackson from the injustice of history, it is all accomplished by building a temple (fane) in the previously untrodden regions of the mourner's mind. "And so it is," writes Jung [16, p. 402]:

> . . . with the hand that guides the crayon or brush, the foot that executes the dance-step, with the eye and the ear, with the word and the thought: a dark impulse is the ultimate arbiter of the pattern, an unconscious *a priori* precipitates itself into plastic form, and one has no inkling that another person's consciousness is being guided by these same principles at the very point where one feels utterly exposed to the boundless subjective vagaries of chance.

The dark impulses which guide creative work are of a kind with the impulses that compel the work of mourning. Just like the writer or artist who sits down to work without knowing in advance exactly what his labors will give birth to, we mourn in suspense of the autonomy of the image. A thought upon waking scribbled into a dream-journal, a fragment of a remembered conversation, a feeling of dread in the pit of the stomach: any of these experiences may be recognized as a call away from life, a call from the beyond. But if we are to find the pattern in the collage of our grief we must actually make the collage.[11]

At the end of the film the Costner character sees his father on the baseball field and suddenly realizes that "Shoeless Joe" was not the person the voice referred to, but only a messenger of this greater one who had now appeared. As is frequently the case in such visions, the father appears in the fullness and vitality of early adulthood. The son approaches the father. Awkwardly, he introduces his wife and daughter to him. Though both are clearly finishing the unfinished business that holds their fates in tandem, neither oppresses the other with infantile demands. Pleased with the baseball diamond which has been built, the father says to the son, "For me, it's like a dream come true." Then the question of life after death is explored more specifically. The father asks the son if they are in heaven. The son replies that they are in "Iowa." "Iowa," repeats the father incredulously, "I could have sworn it was heaven." With the juxtaposition of "Iowa" and "heaven," an identity is implied between the "here" of the bereaved and the "hereafter" of the dead. The two worlds seem to meet at that moment, in the intermediary world of imagination. As Jung suggests in a similar vein [3, pp. 319-320]:

> Psychic existence, and above all the inner images with which we are here concerned, supply the material for all mythic speculations about a life in the hereafter, and I imagine that life as a continuance in the world of images. Thus the psyche might be that existence in which the hereafter or the land of the dead is located.

The dialogue between the father and son continues. Turning to his father, the Costner-character asks him if there is a heaven. As if he had only discovered the answer to this question as a result of what the son had created out of his mourning, the father replies with wonder, conviction, and gratitude: "Oh, yeah! It's the place dreams come true."

[11]"Over the whole procedure there seems to reign a dim foreknowledge not only of the pattern but of its meaning. Image and meaning are identical; and as the first takes shape, so the latter becomes clear. Actually, the pattern needs no interpretation: it portrays its own meaning" [16, p. 204].

JUNG'S TOWER

In 1923, two months after his mother's death, Jung purchased some land in Bollingen on the shore of Lake Zurich. There, at the behest of inner promptings not unlike those which lead the protagonist in "Field of Dreams" to build a baseball diamond, he built a tower out of stone. On the one hand, the Tower was a metaphor for his own personality, a place for himself, "a concretization of the individuation process" [3, p. 225], and on the other hand, it was a place for his ancestors, a place for the dead, a place where their dreams could come true [3, p. 237].

> In the Tower at Bollingen it is as if one lived in many centuries simultaneously. The place will outlive me, and in its location and style it points backward to things of long ago. There is very little about it to suggest the present. If a man of the sixteenth century were to move into the house, only the kerosene lamp and the matches would be new to him. . . . There is nothing to disturb the dead, neither electric light nor telephone. Moreover, my ancestor's souls are sustained by the atmosphere of the house, since I answer for them the questions that their lives once left behind. I carve out rough answers as best I can. I have even drawn them on the walls. It is as if a silent, greater family, stretching down the centuries, were peopling the house. There I . . . see life in the round, as something forever coming into being and passing on. [3, p. 237]

Over the years, Jung added a number of extensions to the Tower, each intended to make place for what had previously felt excluded in his own personality. In addition, when images and ideas came to him as if from the dead he attempted to carve them into the stone walls or to paint them. After his wife's death, for instance, Jung chiseled the names of his paternal ancestors onto three stone tablets and painted motifs from the coats of arms of his family, his wife's family, and the families of his sons-in-law [3, p. 00].

> When I was working on the stone tablets, I became aware of the fateful links between me and my ancestors. I feel very strongly that I am under the influence of things or questions which were left incomplete and unanswered by my parents and grandparents and more distant ancestors. It often seems as if there were an

> impersonal karma within a family, which is passed on from parents to children.

Commenting on the importance of the living taking up the problems of the dead, Jung continues [3, pp. 234-235]:

> It is difficult to determine if these questions [of the dead] are more of a personal or more of a general (collective) nature. It seems to me that the latter is the case. A collective problem, if not recognized as such, always appears as a personal problem, and in individual cases may give the impression that something is out of order in the realm of the personal psyche. The personal sphere is indeed disturbed, but such disturbances need not be primary; they may well be secondary, the consequence of an insupportable change in the social atmosphere. The cause of the disturbance is, therefore, not to be sought in the personal surroundings, but rather in the collective situation.

In this passage Jung is not simply saying that our seemingly personal problems prove often to be collective—that we are canaries in a coal mine. He is saying as well that the unresolved issues which our forebears present to us in personal form were and are collective problems for them too. Our lost loved ones inhabit the purgatory of the archetypal dilemmas which they were unable to resolve. While in life they may have seemed a motley crew, in their death and absence, they present us with a greater significance, a more archetypal necessity. In the Kingdom of Ends they operate as categories, active intelligences, inquisitive angels. Through them the eternal questions of man and the transpersonal aspects of existence take on personal form. They ask our help to solve the riddles which the gods have posed for them. Jung's father's personal fatality, for example, brought the whole, collective Christian problem home to Jung in a personal manner. He saw his father as a canary in the coal mine of an incomplete religious spirit and set about in his many writings to heal the wider spiritual problem which was his father's ruin.[12]

[12]Murray Stein, in a fuller discussion of this theme, writes: "While Paul Jung suffered the spiritual plight of modern man dumbly and blindly, his son Carl Gustav would take it on as a conscious problem in desperate need of resolution. Healing the spiritual sources of his father's suffering became in many ways Jung's vocation" [17, p. 24].

LE CRI DE MERLIN

The analogy between Jung's building a tower for the dead at Bollingen and the protagonist in the "Field of Dreams" building a baseball diamond for them, is further underlined by Jung's notion of "*Le Cri de Merlin.*" Just as in the film a voice implores the Iowa farmer to build a place to which the dead may come, Jung states in his autobiography that the meaning of the Tower he built at Bollingen is epitomized by the legend, which dates back to the twelfth century, of the sorcerer Merlin, whose voice continued to haunt the forests after he left the world. It is believed that people right up to the present day still hear his cries, though they are unable to understand them. Jung comments that Merlin represents a compensation on the part of the "medieval unconscious" to the Christian hero, Parsifal. The son of the devil and a pure virgin, Merlin, in Jung's view, presents the shadow of Christianity's Parsifalian ideal. The fact that no one understood the cry implies that consciousness again fell out of contact with the values Merlin personified and that "he lives on in an unredeemed form" [3, p. 228]. Jung felt that the Merlin story, which in the most general terms is about living on close terms with the mercurial spirit of the unconscious, is not finished. Though alchemy adopted Merlin in the form of Mercurius and Jung took him up again in his psychology of the unconscious, his cry can still be heard [3, p. 228].

JUNG'S DEATH

According to his closest associates, Jung frequently dreamt that a replica of his tower stood on the other side of the lake from where it had actually been erected. He understood this dream to be a revelation of the tower's true form in the Beyond.[13] The tower which he had built was merely the earthly copy of this other-worldly home for the soul. Lawrence's notion of building the "Ship of Death" is reminiscent here. Jung, in building his tower at Bollingen, was also "build[ing] [a] ship of death to carry [his] soul on the longest journey," the journey into death and the hereafter. Two months before he died, Jung dreamt of his tower once more. This time it was entirely made of gold and he

[13]Stated in Jung's own psychological terms, the tower on the other side of the lake would be an image of the Self.

seemed to come to it from an unknown place. A voice in the tower told him it was completed and ready for habitation.[14] He was ready to die.

LIVING IN THE EVER-AFTER

What do the dead want? This question, which haunts the mourning process, also underpins our conceptualization of the meaning of life. It is not merely that our attitudes toward death shape our attitudes toward life. More than that, it is our particularized awareness of the dead which underpins a particularized awareness of our own lives. Death is not only the great leveller. To the heart that mourns it is also the great particularizer. Death lends definition to our roots. We come to appreciate how we are rooted in each other and grow out of one another. Death is the common heritage which holds the generations together. The task of each new generation is to aerate this soil, that is, to address the past in a manner that allows the present to be lived more fully and the future to be anticipated more meaningfully. We must imagine past the Reaper with his scythe to the actual souls which are Death's harvest. Behind the grim frown there is a richness in death, a richness that can be found only by mourning. Living hands reach out of the grave toward us, as Keats said in the poem at the beginning of this chapter.

It is tempting to turn away from our ancestors and to resign from culture, like an adolescent rebelling against the older generation. The result of this, however, is a life so shallow that it kills the soul. Rather than flee the determining weight of the past into an existence which is unbearably light, we must build, each of us in our own souls, a new man or new woman who, while being discontinuous with the past, is also related to it enough to partake in its redemption. Like Joyce writing about his native Ireland, we too, each in our own small way, must "forge in the smithy of [our] soul[s] the uncreated conscience of [our] race" [19, p. 253].

[14]Other details of this dream are of interest. Jung found the golden tower to be a place of utter loneliness and silence. There were no people anywhere. But then, down by the water, a mother wolverine could be seen teaching its cub to swim in the water. Von Franz, whose reading of this dream I have been following above, interprets this last part to mean that just as "Mother Nature adapts and accustoms her children to life through their instincts, so an instinct will likewise help us to adapt to the altered conditions in the Beyond" [18, p. 130].

REFERENCES

1. D. Perkins (ed)., *English Romantic Writers*, Harcourt Brace Jovanovich, New York, 1967.
2. D. Eddy, Completing Brad's Dreams, in *The Family Therapy Networker*, September-October, R. Simon (ed.), 1986.
3. C. G. Jung, *Memories, Dreams, Reflections*, A. Jaffe (ed.), R. & C. Winston, (trans.), Random House, New York, 1961.
4. W. Blake, *Selected Poetry and Prose of Blake*, N. Frye (ed.), Random House, New York, 1953.
5. H. Kalweit, *Dreamtime and Inner Space*, Shambhala, Boston, 1988.
6. A. Jaffe, *Apparitions: An Archetypal Approach to Death Dreams and Ghosts*, Spring Publications, Dallas, 1978.
7. W. Barnstone (ed.), *The Other Bible*, Harper & Row, New York, 1984.
8. J. Campbell, *The Masks of God: Primitive Mythology*, Viking Press, New York, 1959.
9. M. Eliade, *The Sacred and the Profane*, W. Trask (trans.), Harcourt Brace & World, New York, 1959.
10. R. Woodman, Blake as Milton's Pastoral Counsellor, forthcoming in *The Journal of Pastoral Counselling*, 1991.
11. M. Kundera, *The Unbearable Lightness of Being*, M. H. Heim (trans.), Harper & Row, New York, 1985.
12. T. S. Eliot, *Collected Poems 1909-1962*, Farber & Farber, London, 1974.
13. J. Bowlby, *Attachment and Loss, Volume III, Loss: Sadness and Depression*, Penguin Books, Harmondsworth, 1985.
14. *Field of Dreams*, P. A. Robinson (screen play and direction), 1989.
15. J. Keats, Ode to Psyche, in *John Keats: Selected Poems and Letters*, D. Bush (ed.), Houghton Mifflin, Boston, 1959.
16. C. G. Jung, *The Structure and Dynamics of the Psyche, Collected Works*, Vol. 8., R. F. C. Hull (trans.), Princeton University Press, Princeton, 1960.
17. M. Stein, The Significance of Jung's Father in His Destiny as a Therapist of Christianity, in *Quadrant: Journal of the C. G. Jung Foundation for Analytical Psychology*, *18*:1, 1985
18. M-L. Von Franz, *On Dreams and Death*, E. X. Kennedy (trans.), Shambala, Boston, 1987.
19. J. Joyce, *A Portrait of the Artist as a Young Man*, Penguin, Harmondsworth, 1988.

11.17.07

CHAPTER 8

Mourning and Culture

> Death is the side of life averted from us, unshone upon by us: we must try to achieve the greatest consciousness of our existence which is at home in both unbounded realms, inexhaustibly nourished from both. . . . The true figure of life extends through both spheres, the blood of the mightiest circulation flows through both: there is neither a here nor a beyond, but the great unity in which the beings that surpass us, the 'angels,' are at home. . . . We of the here and now are not for a moment hedged in the time-world, nor confined within it; we are incessantly flowing over and over to those who preceded us. . . . We are the bees of the invisible. *Nous butinons eperdument le miel du visible, pour l'accumuler dans la grande ruche d'or de l'Invisible* [1, pp. 373-374].
>
> Rilke

THE BLAMEFUL CHILD

The main traditions of psychotherapy conceptualize the therapeutic enterprise in terms of the needs of the living. Therapy encourages its patients to free themselves from the fetters of the past, to grow and to change. The journey towards health and happiness is frequently imagined as a journey away from home. When the past is examined, it is often done negatively, in the spirit of blame. Fathers are construed as absent, mothers as overinvolved. Increasingly, psychotherapy sees the child—even in the adult patient—as the victim of his or her forebears [2].

Partly, this is a function of our contemporary cult of childhood. Central to this cult is the belief that children are infinitely imaginative and limitlessly creative.[1] The alleged loss of this capacity for creativity and imagination as we grow up we tend to blame on our parents and their unempathic childrearing practices. It has become fashionable in recent times to think of ourselves no longer as mature adults, but as the "adult-children" of parents who have traumatized us. Somehow, through some deficit in parenting or misuse of the world and its resources, they have ruined our lives.

Of course, there is no denying that parents throughout history have made mistakes. The enormous attention which has been given to these mistakes in the last two decades has shown that parents today are no less culpable. But blame is nothing new either: it is as old as the Garden of Eden, where the "children"—Adam and Eve—established a chain of blame that led back ultimately to God, the "parent" of the human race. However, as history has taught us, blame is of little value in dealing constructively with human problems.

One way to deal constructively with the parent/child standoff is to repunctuate the situation so that the blameful child in us may realize that responsibility is a matter of perspective. If we find ourselves poor in spirit and limited in imagination it is not because our parents stifled our creativity (though this they may have done) but because we have failed to respond creatively to their apparent mishandling of us. Thus, it is not our parents themselves but our reactive relationship to them that impoverishes us.

Even if they have abused us—physically, emotionally, sexually—blame does little to set things right. Important as it is to recognize their culpability in order to redeem them, we must not use their blameworthiness as an excuse not to grow up ourselves. Accusing our parents, rather than dealing creatively with the problems their lives have posed for us, renders us sterile and empty.

LIFE WITHOUT DEATH

Perhaps the underlying reason we blame our lives on our parents is that the life they gave to us includes death. Wanting to live a life of unlimited growth and expansion, we view the natural process of death and decay as something wrong. Rather than learning from our parents and ancestors how to live into death, and even beyond it in a spiritual

[1] For an in-depth examination of the shadows of the child-archetype see a work by James Hillman [3, pp. 5-48].

sense, we attempt to create away from death, and thereby away from life as well. But playing with the technological toys of the 20th century is a poor substitute for the mourning process.

Unable to imagine life in a manner that embraces death, we devotees of the cult of childhood dedicate our creative efforts to suppressing our awareness of death and to its deferral. Obsessed with youth and youthfulness we are committed to finding ever new ways to keep the Grim Reaper at bay. Modern medicine, for instance, in its zeal to delay death, has developed the technology to transplant organs, shrink tumors, and create replacement body parts from fetal tissue. No one today is considered too old or too sick to be kept alive on a respirator or to be a candidate for surgery. Even if a patient is certain to die, the attempt to keep him alive is considered worthwhile, since it may advance the science of prolonging life. The relatively recent techniques of cosmetic surgery help us to keep the specter of death away in a similar manner. The face-lift and the tummy tuck, the nose job and the breast implants allow us to look and feel younger than we actually are, thereby creating the illusion of having slowed down the aging process. Genetic engineering also offers hope of longer, healthier, "happier" lives. Through the manipulation of genetic material, medical researchers hope to find ways to control diseases which speed up aging and death.

Caught up in these technologies of youth and longevity we have almost entirely lost our awareness of our own mortality. But when life is not lived as a quest for the meanings and values that prepare it for death it becomes more and more empty. Though this emptiness, if pondered, could restore our relationship to death, it too is denied. In a pathetic attempt to fill our lives with something we redouble our commitment to the very activities which made them empty in the first place. The vicious circle which then develops is like the downward spiral of an addiction. Afraid of death, we become dependent on the technologies that appear to protect us from it. More jogging, more face-lifts, more vitamins, and more medical interventions become necessary at a time when we can no longer imagine anything important enough to suffer or die for. Kept alive beyond our natural span by the artificial means at our disposal, "quarantined" from the reality of death, we are unable to feel the necessity of creating for ourselves a vehicle that will carry us into the Beyond, a soul.

Technologies that invent without reference to the dead and their questions have a de-humanizing effect. Gradually, we become more and more like the machines which we hope will keep death away. While in earlier times we worshipped our ancestors, philosophized in the face of death, and gained knowledge of the soul, today our heads, like our computers, are cluttered with trivial information. Cluttered, trivialized minds create for creation's sake only, without the perspective of the past, the future be damned. Ironically, however, creating *ex nihilo*—out of nothing—instead of out of ancestors, places us squarely in the midst of the abyss. More and more invention and consumption becomes necessary to create the illusion of content and to mask the emptiness. We can only hope that future generations will be able to free themselves and us from this ruinous identification with the child-archetype and to rediscover the true meaning of Christ's remark "Unless you turn and become like children, you will never enter the kingdom of heaven" (Matt. 18: 3).

THE BANKRUPTCY OF THE TRADITION

Even when dealing specifically with issues of loss and bereavement, psychotherapy tends to ignore the dead. Mourning tends to be conceptualized first and foremost as a parting and letting-go. The therapist experiences the bereaved as bankrupt and depleted by their loss, and empathizes with their desolation. Of course, this is helpful and necessary—especially in the beginning. The bereaved feel supported by the empathic statements which the therapist makes in this vein. Basic human needs are met by this generic sharing of heart. At a deeper level, however, this kind of empathic response is not entirely appropriate. The *desolation* of the bereaved is not wholly a function of the loss of a dear one, but of the bankrupt culture in which that loss is being experienced. Indeed, even before they have lost their loved ones, the bereaved, especially in modern times, are already bereft of the supernatural containers, the religious and spiritual ideas, that could provide their loved ones a place of repose in the Beyond.

One of the great tragedies of our time, unfolding before our very eyes, is the "epidemic" of cultural illiteracy sweeping across North America among our children. Suckled at television's electronic breast, they have grown up on a diet of inanity and gratuitous violence. Their heros, Hulk Hogan, the Grateful Dead, and RoboCop have nothing significant to say on the subject of loss and death. How does a child make room for such things in a world peopled by such vacuous characters? Furthermore, when this child eventually meets death, how will she take her place in the pantheon of the ancestor gods: gods whom she never knew?

Modernity is rapidly coming to be identified as a state of discontinuity with the past. The Existentialists foreshadowed this. They even saw its outcome, and called it *angst*. The effeteness and bankruptcy in our culture, the source of our *angst*, is captured exquisitely in T. S. Eliot's "The Hollow Men." He portrays our world as a "dead land," a "cactus land," where we raise the "stone images" of our culture—our thoroughly modern, "totally radical" yet utterly useless heroes. He then goes on to say:

> In death's other kingdom
> Waking alone
> At the hour when we are
> Trembling with tenderness
> Lips that would kiss
> Form prayers to broken stone [4, p. 90-91].

What a poignant portrayal of modern man, waking up after death in the hereafter, and longing to greet the ancestors with a kiss, but only being able to call upon his "broken stone" heroes in vain! Eliot saw that if we lost our sense of the ancestral dimension of the soul, we would grieve our loved ones and face our own death with a sense of "quiet desperation."

LOCATING THE DEAD IN CULTURE

Mourning is a less desolate process when it is supported by culture. Though the pain of loss may remain acute, the meaning supplied by our faith and tradition may help it to be borne. It is not just that we will let go of the dead more easily if we have beliefs which help us to retain their essences. The process is more circular than that. Our concept of the soul is substantiated by death. We believe in the afterlife because our love persists beyond the decease of our loved ones. Mourning is as supportive of an unseen order as it is supported by it. In bereavement, our losses become incorporated into the spirit we live from, making that spirit—for better or for worse—more vital. The dead, for their part, create culture even as they inhabit it, providing us with metaphors of their return as containers for our grief.

Jesus' remark to a bereaved man in the Gospels is a good illustration of this point. On his final journey to Jerusalem, Jesus came upon a man and said to him, "Follow me," The man, however, wished to bury his deceased father first. Replying to the bereaved son's request, Jesus said, "Allow the dead to bury their own dead; but as for you, go and proclaim everywhere the kingdom of God" (Luke 9: 60). Although to the modern, secularized ear this comment seems brutally insensitive, Jesus was not being callous. On the contrary, he was admonishing the bereaved son to prepare the way for his father's induction into the Kingdom of God by "go[ing] and proclaim[ing] everywhere" that Kingdom. Burying the father would only widen "the Great Divide" that now separated the father from the son, for they would dwell in two discontinuous worlds: the son in the "upper" world of the living, the father in the "nether" world of the dead. Proclaiming the Kingdom, on the other hand, would establish a place that both father and son could inhabit simultaneously, though one was dead and the other alive. What this really amounts to, then, is a facilitation of the father's resurrection on the part of the son. While Burial separates,[2] the kingdom of God reunites.

As Kohut has pointed out, death constellates the disintegration anxiety we first felt as children when we were separated from our parents. Burial serves to magnify this anxiety. Christ's strategy was to undermine the power of this anxiety by an act of symbolic abandonment on the part of the one who feels abandoned. This active abandonment by the bereaved is done in the secure knowledge that the dead are not being abandoned to nothing: they are being abandoned to the welcoming arms of the already dead.

By his own death and resurrection, Christ cast death in an entirely different light and gave it a whole new meaning. In breaking "death's strong bands" he liberated his contemporaries psychologically from the power of death, freeing the living to live this life "more abundantly," and freeing the dead to preside more actively over the affairs of the Kingdom. Christ's good news for the dead was that in dying they had conquered death: they were no longer subject to it. With Paul they exclaim: "O death, where is thy sting? O grave, where is thy victory?" (1 Cor. 15: 55). It is in being completely beyond the reach of death that the dead are immortal, and this realization has a profound significance

[2] Notice that Christ said: "*Allow* the dead to bury their own dead," implying that burial is rightfully performed by the dead, not the living. He seems to be saying that the living hinder the dead in the performance of their proper tasks when they [the living] insist on performing the burial. Burial by the living is an act of separation from the ancestor: a farewell. Burial by the dead, however, is an act of reunion with the ancestors: a welcome. In an archetypal sense it is Christ himself, who, having been slain from the foundation of the world (1 Pet, 1: 19, 20) and thus become the "firstborn of the dead" (Rev. 1: 5. 1 Cor. 15: 20), performs the burial of the dead by the dead.

for the living. It is this radical reinterpretation of death that must be seen as the basis for the new dispensation.

With his enigmatic remark on the burial of the dead Christ made the new dispensation, into which he was inviting the bereaved son, inclusive and redemptive of the old dispensation, to which the deceased father belonged. Stated in psychological terms, the "old dispensation" is the "childish," blame-oriented approach to the dead. In this approach we make our deceased loved ones bear the blame for our inadequacies just as the sacrificer in the old dispensation projected his "sins" onto the sacrificial animal, the proverbial "scapegoat." In the more "adult" approach of the "new dispensation," however, the people we mourn can no longer stand in for us on the altar of life. Just as Christ in the new dispensation as "Passover Lamb," "takes away the sins of the world" (John 1: 29), so the "adult" approach takes away the blame.

The veil of the temple was rent from top to bottom at the death of Christ, rendering the forms of the old dispensation ineffective. If the bereaved son is to do anything for his dead father he must do so from within the new spiritual order which Christ has inaugurated. The souls of the dead do not simply rest in the old dispensation as if in heaven; heaven is something that we must proclaim to them from our new cultural ground even as Christ preached to the dead in *Gehenna*.

In the new dispensation, the bereaved son is not an abandoned child, nor is his deceased father an unmourned soul. On the contrary, the dead father lives on in the afterlife which the son has helped to establish by creating beyond him. Though loss constellates the abandoned child, the experience of mourning need not be confined to the perspective if its archetypal neediness. On the contrary, the mourner can experience his loss as a call bidding him to take on the initiative for his own life. The meaning of the mourning process resides in the making of culture. The Kingdom of God for which the living son may seem to forsake the dead father is, for the Christian at least, the very container of the mourning process.

PUBERTY RITES AT THE GRAVESIDE

The abandonment feelings and regressive behavior that can accompany the mourning process have less to do with a reluctance to relinquish a loved or not-so-loved one than with a reluctance to relinquish what has been or become childish (Freud would say, narcissistic) about our attachment to them. While in traditional societies young people are initiated into their adult lives through rites which symbolically put to death their childish identity so that an adult personality can form, in our society the initiatory encounter with death may come to us for the very first time only in adulthood through the loss of someone dear. The boy who has been taken into the men's house at puberty, beaten up, circumcised, symbolically killed, and told the tribal mythologies and tales of the ancestors mourns more maturely than the man of today, who has not undergone initiation, and therefore, is still a child. In modern society, the last rite of passage—the initiation of the dead into death—is attenuated by the mourner's lack of initiation. The unfinished business which the bereaved need to complete with the dead is a function of their own failure to grow up. Death hurls into relief all that has been missed. Tragically, at forty or fifty, we still need from our deceased parents what society failed to provide us when we were thirteen or fourteen.

If evolution's maxim—ontogeny recapitulates phylogeny—is correct, then what is true in regard to the lack of initiation on the individual level is also true on the phylogenetic level of the human race. It became fashionable, during the heyday of "God-is-dead" theology, to speak of modern man as "man come of age." But if the "coming of age" of the individual is a paradigm for the "coming of age" of the human race, then we have little to brag about. If indeed the human race has come of age, it has done so without the benefit of an initiation, and is the poorer for it. It seems as though two world wars were not enough to initiate us into death. Perhaps we require something on a much larger scale to help us grow up as a race.

Today, for the first time in human history, the human race, collectively, is mourning for a dying planet. The fate of the earth depends upon our understanding the dynamics of the mourning process. Though it is tempting to lament the fate of the earth and blame our forebears for its present state, we must put these childish sentiments aside and take up the adult task of re-visioning our ancestral inheritance and educating the dead. Rather than fleeing the problems of global warming and pollution, war and overpopulation by blaming the Enlightenment and the Industrial Revolution, we must recognize these as the initiatory ordeals that kill the self-preoccupied child in us in order to implant in its place the full, adult generativity of global citizenship.

The failure of modern society to provide us individually with rites of initiation may itself be seen as initiatory on a collective level. The "calamity" which we inherit is, as Baha'u'llah, the prophet of world citizenship, noted, "our providence." "While outwardly [it may appear to be] fire and vengeance, inwardly it is light and mercy." The dead did not know that they were bringing calamity upon the globe. It is up to us now to turn that calamity into providence, in the true spirit of mourning, by taking hold of the living hand our ancestors extend toward us and learning from their mistakes. It is tragic, but perhaps necessary, that the human race must undergo its rites of adulthood at the graveside of the planet.

INITIATING MOURNING

A danger associated with loss and bereavement, as with all the other tribulations of life, is that the mourner will try to evade the anxiety that attends a loss and thereby affirm a smaller personality. Rather than being initiated by loss and living more fully in the face of death, the mourner may shrink from death, and thereby, from life as well. Instead of setting aside childish attitudes and taking on the wider issues which his loss bequeaths to him, he may try to preserve his previous identity.

Therapy's chief task is to prevent the mourner from construing loss in a manner that will create a personality deficit. Though the troubled mourner may view the decease of a dear one as abandonment, punishment, betrayal or torture, the therapist must help him to view these throes of grief as necessary features of the initiatory ordeal we call the mourning process. Though at first it may be necessary for the bereaved to rail against the anxiety the deceased pass on to them, this is essentially a preliminary stage to their eventually taking this anxiety on themselves. The unfinished business which the bereaved have—the anger and rage, the blame and regret—resolves itself when the childish tie to the dead is severed and a mature bond is forged. Though therapy must facilitate whatever rites of initiation have been postponed from earlier life stages, the actual work of mourning is accomplished by the bereaved replying to the lives of the dead through an increased vitality in their own living. It makes no difference whether they loved them or hated them: to be fully generative, the bereaved must make soul with the dead. This is the subtext of Sophocles' tragedy *Antigone*, in which Creon, the king, bans this process with disastrous results.

EGO, SELF, AND DEATH

The bereaved experience death differently from different psychological vantage points. From the point of view of the ego, death is dumb, senseless and cruel. Someone we love has been snatched away from us and our lives are the poorer for it. From the point of view of the Self, however, death may be experienced as a "joyous event." "In the light of eternity," writes Jung commenting on this latter view [5, p. 314],

> [Death] is a wedding, a *mysterium coniunctionis*. The soul attains, as it were, its missing half, it achieves wholeness. On Greek sarcophagi the joyous element was represented by dancing girls, on Etruscan tombs by banquets. When the pious Cabbalist Rabbi Simon ben Jochai came to die, his friends said that he was celebrating his wedding. To this day it is the custom in many regions to hold a picnic on the graves on All Soul's Day. Such customs express the feeling that death is really a festive occasion.

Though Jung stresses only positive images in this passage, the Self's vision of the afterlife may also be darker and more purgatorial. The actual status of the dead in the hereafter is independent of the idealizing nature of memory. Hades is not an ideal world. Nor is *Sheol* or *Gehenna*. Though the Christian afterlife holds the promise of heaven, its holds other possibilities as well: limbo, purgatory, and hell. At death our dear and not-so-dear ones are gathered to their imagery. They take up residence in the inscapes of their own souls. For some this is a far from heavenly end. The dead are not ideal images, but subtle bodies. When they appear to us in a negative manner, as, for instance, the souls of the unredeemed, they do so not merely from the ego's point of view. Such experiences can be a function of the point of view of the Self. The ego confronts us with the fact that we have lost someone; the Self, on the other hand, confronts us with the problem of the meaning and salvation of a loss.

While empathizing with the ego's sense of loss, it is important that the therapist not become wholly identified with it. At the same time as he helps the bereft mourner to face the reality of a loss and to bear the unbearable feelings associated with it, he must also be sensitive to the psychological richness that is latent in the mourning process. As soon as possible the therapist must bring the deceased into the conversation, and thereby into the room. The mourner will recognize and appreciate the fact that the therapist cannot fully understand him without knowing more about the loved one he has lost. Details, stories, photographs: together the mourner and therapist must partake of the fruits of the dear one's life—picnic on the grave. It is by empathizing precisely, that is, by asking for precise descriptions of the lost loved one, that the perspective of the Self begins to emerge.

THE RICHNESS OF DEATH

In their absence, the dead continue to exert an influence. No matter how bitterly we experience our loss of them, we are the richer for having known them. In subtle ways, the life we once shared together deepens our own ongoing life. Our experience of having known them provides us a context for further experiencing. The life that we continue to live becomes a cultured life, a life informed by instances of life lost, a life informed by death. As all this is appreciated in the therapy, the mourner's soul becomes more and more robust.

After a death, we no longer exist exclusively for ourselves or even for our living companions. The loss of a loved one deepens our relationship to the species in general. The parts of ourselves which were revealed to us by the person who is now dead are rendered "timeless" and preside like a conscience over the life we live in time. We begin to feel an increased sense of responsibility, a responsibility to the futurity of the life that the dead made possible.

The dead are metapsychological. The lineaments of their desires—both gratified and ungratified—give our psyche its basic shape. The ways in which they fulfilled or defaulted on their lives is a major determinant of our psychic structure. It is not so much a question of the genetics of our forebears or even of the domestic values by which they raised us—the so-called nature/nurture controversy. Our psychic constitution is a function of their deaths. The first five years of our lives are not as important as the two million years that underpin their deaths. Who they were for us matters less than who they were for themselves at the end. Individuation is a multi-generational family affair. Nothing affects us more than the incompleteness of our forebears' lives. Our attitudes toward life are haunted by their deaths: We see it from the vantage point of their end state. The imagery to which they have been gathered encapsulates our own imaginations. In depression we see from their purgatorial perspective, in joy from their heavenly viewpoint.

Freud's speculations on the origins of life are noteworthy in this context. As we have already discussed in Chapter One, Freud assigned to death a key role in the development of life. In *Beyond the Pleasure Principle*, a monograph on metapsychology written in the style of a creation myth, Freud suggests that life forms owe their expansion and differentiation to cells which, having been killed by the perturbing energies of the external world, assume an inorganic form and protect "all the deeper [living] layers from a similar fate" [6, p. 21]. Though Freud here refers to the dead cells which form the crust, skins, scales, shells and hides that protect all living creatures, we could also apply it to our deceased forebears. They, too, form a protective layer around the living.

As a tortoise lives inside the dead cells that make up its shell, we dwell metapsychologically in our ancestors. It is not so much that we bury them in culture, although this is true enough. In a deeper sense, *they* are the culture in which *we* are protectively contained. Though Freud employed the notion of the dead cells as an analogy to explain his metapsychological framework, we can take the analogy quite literally. To say that the dead function as the epidermis of the psyche is not to speak metaphorically so much as to grant to this metaphor, to other images of the dead, and to the imagination in general,[3] this particular protective function.

As we discussed in Chapter One, Freud ascribes yet another function to the dead cells: perception. Though the outer cells have been killed by the stimuli impinging upon them from the outer world, they can, in their dead form, serve to filter and reduce the intensity of the stimuli that killed them, rendering these stimuli available for sensation by the deeper, living layers. Not only do the dead protect us from the forces at large in the universe, they facilitate our perception of those forces. We see more clearly than they did the forces that killed them, because their deaths provide us with a context and a perspective.

Of course, culture does not protect us completely. Though the dead shield us from the events that killed them and provide us a clearer perception, we are still vulnerable to events which "break through the protective shield" [6, p. 21]. Like our deceased forebears, we, too, will encounter events which kill our personalities and make us into characters. And just as the hardening of our parents against the overwhelming events of their lives protected our generation and made way for its insights, so our eventual demise will be a richness we in turn pass on to our children.

[3] For a fuller account of the protective function of metaphor see an earlier work of my own [7, pp. 93-112].

THE CULTURING INFLUENCE OF THE DEAD

The mourning of a loss brings about a culturalization of the soul. Whatever we continue to love beyond the grave joins the community of the dead and becomes an ancestor of consciousness. Though we may have previously believed the mind to be a *tabula rasa*, the mourning process teaches us otherwise. It is not just that our souls become more and more deeply inscribed with each loss. The depths of the psyche reach back phylogentically to the first losses which, at the dawn of time, made consciousness possible. Just as Adam, the mythical first man, is the progenitor of human life, so his son Abel—the first person ever to die—is the mythical progenitor of the human soul. The mourning of our loved ones, though personal, has archetypal reaches. Inside the grief of the bereaved we see the markings on the cave wall.

Although we may feel desolate and alone in our grief, the mourning process is far from solitary. We are assisted in our bereavement by the community of the dead. Each of our losses resonates with the entire history of loss, constellating, thereby, the archetypes which structure the rites associated with death. We do not invent the mourning process by ourselves. It is bequeathed to us by our departed dear ones and ancestors. We merely rediscover it for ourselves through our dialogue with death.

Foreknowledge of this inheritance—Jung called it the collective unconscious—is not necessary. Wise Hades supplies us with the wherewithal to grieve. Just as Socrates led the slave boy to an awareness of knowledge he did not know he had, Death draws up from the depths of our grief the necessary guidance for its mysteries. Though consciously held religious ideas about the afterlife assist the bereaved, the mourning process can supply such ideas spontaneously to those who are bereft of them. In the dreams and visions of the bereaved not only the mourned return, the spirits of long-dead friends and relatives "speed from their sepulchers" to assist in the process as well. In this way the mourning of a dear one can open the mourner up to a wider sense of the soul's culture.

DREAMING OF DEATH AND WAKING TO CULTURE

A widow dreamt that her husband was alive again and in the company of her long-dead father. Neither of the men knew that he was dead. Also present were relatives unknown to her. The next day she awakened to the perspective of the ego and the grief of their absence.

A young man whose father was terminally ill dreamt that there was to be a family reunion. Many long-dead relatives would be in attendance. Upon entering his parents' house the dream-ego found that it had been broken into by a mysterious lady in white and by a man who reminded him of Richard Burton in "The Medusa Touch"—the archetypal figure of Death himself. Though he had previously not given any particular consideration to the afterlife, the archetypal features of this and other dreams he had during his father's illness suggested to him that some kind of continuation after death might be possible.

Thus, the dreams of the bereft and of those anticipating bereavement present images suggestive of a life in the hereafter. Classical motifs of mourning, such as home fires being extinguished, the donning of mourning veils or sackcloth, shoes worn upon the head, and awakening in the night to the singing of a bird, may suggest to the dreamer, if he considers their archetypal significance, that his grief is part of a larger, transpersonal pattern of meaning and purpose.

Sometimes dreams presage the decease of a loved one and embroil the dreamer in the drama of death. The White Lady appears weeks before the death is anticipated in waking life. Blood seeps out of the top of a mourner's doorway, as if to prevent the Angel of Death from claiming him too. A fault in the ground near the sea wall opens wide, creating an island in the beyond. Barns full of fruit and granaries full of wheat present images of the Reaper's harvest. The dreamer senses the relative completeness of the dear one's life. The grain, which is also seed, inspires reveries of death and rebirth.

Dreams that presage death can often be quite uncanny [8]. In psychotherapeutic practice one frequently meets dreamers who are burdened by dreams which predict death with great accuracy.[4] In many cases the dreamer recognizes a particular dream-motif which is suggestive of death and which is invariably followed by the actual decease of someone in the vicinity. While persons who have frequent portents of death are often very oppressed by them, precognitive experiences

[4] Why a person should have this "gift" is not clear. A patient of mine who has frequently had precognitive dreams which presage death lost her mother as a young child. In a manner of speaking, this woman has been mothered by death. In addition, having been raised by relatives who she felt did not actually want her, she never completely "incarnated" into these new relationships to the extent that they could replace the bonding with the absent mother. If perception is in some sense a function of loss, as I suggested in chapter one, then perhaps the dead mother is the organ of perception that makes these precognitive experiences possible. Of course, this is only a suggestion: my attempt to create, as Jung recommends, a "myth of the dead" from the data of dreams.

can also be reassuring. In a letter to a correspondent who had written to him regarding dreams she had had which anticipated her mother's death, Jung commented that such dreams have "objective significance and by all human standards must be regarded as messages" [9, pp. 371-372]. Jung uses the words "human standards" here because he recognizes that he is not making a scientific judgement. In Jung's view, the dreamer should value her experience in terms of the meanings it can contribute to her myth of death. As he concludes at the end of the letter, such messages are "wonderful and [make] for reconciliation" [9, p. 372].

The dreams of the dying must be mentioned in this context as well. Marie-Louise Von Franz, in her excellent book *On Dreams and Death*, writes of a terminally ill man who dreamt that a bright gleam of light streamed in through the window and that an ominous stranger suddenly appeared in the room [10, p. 68]. Another experience reported in the same work is that of a dying woman who was reassured of the ongoing life of the soul by a dream of a candle being extinguished and then lighting itself again on the other side of the window pane [10, p. 64]. Darker images are also common. The dying may dream of dark holes in the ground and unpleasant purgatorial resting places. Trees and scrubs may be burned away in an all-consuming fire from which something may or may not emerge unscathed. Death may take on a decidedly religious flavor. A young boy dying of leukemia, who was bereft of any religious culture whatsoever until his aunt told him the story of Christ in the last days of his life, saw Jesus at his door welcoming him to a feast in Paradise. Angels may also play the psychopompic role, like the angel who rolled the rock away to reveal the empty tomb of Christ. Those facing martyrdom, both male and female, have sometimes experienced near-death ecstasies in which they were married to the divine bridegroom.

And then there are the images of the deceased themselves. After a loved one has died, the bereaved may continue to dream of him or her. The dead may return in youthful, reassuring shapes. They may even appear to have obtained the freedom, in their liberated state, to pursue the interests that were their heart's desire but that they were unable to pursue in life. The souls of other loved ones, however, may return in a more unresolved aspect. Forlorn and unredeemed, they may dwell uneasily in "Pluto's substanceless Empire" of dreams. Just as the personifications of human malediction—Grief, Resentful Care, Old Age, Fear, Hunger, Poverty, Sin, Death, War and Strife—reside in the "Jaws of Hades," so the underworld of the mourner may be crowded with the souls of those who died without having sufficiently individuated themselves from these conditions. Haunted by the issues and problems their lost loved ones found impossible to resolve in their own lives, the bereaved may experience a particularly oppressive sense of grief. Still clutching a whisky bottle, the shade of a long-dead mother continues to upset her grieving children until their emotional ties are sufficiently mortified. A dreamer finds himself subject to worries about the status of a lost friend in the afterlife, in spite of his rationalistic prejudice against even considering the possibility of a hereafter. Gradually, however, his dreams of the dead supply him with a mythical formulation which can contain his grief and permit him to mourn in a manner congruent with the actual psychic and emotional issues which entwine his fate with that of the deceased.

INTERPRETATION

> When we are alive our souls are dead and buried in us, but when we die they come alive again and live.
>
> Heraclitus

The stirrings of culture can begin through just these kinds of experiences. Without any interpretation the dreams may even speak for themselves. As the bereaved move back and forth from the perspective of the waking ego to that of the dreaming Self their grief gradually becomes absorbed into a larger sense of meaning. When facilitating the process through dreamwork, the therapist must take care not to abort these soul-making or death-making processes with reductive interpretations. What is important is that the bereaved experience the autonomy of the images which animate the mourning process, the autonomy of the dead. As they awaken to an awareness of the culture of the unconscious, the ability of the dead to bury the dead, they will sense themselves to be citizens of a timeless realm of meaning, inhabitants of a Kingdom.

Although the bereaved may benefit from interpretation on the subjective level, thereby gaining insight into the personal complexes and emotions which the dead continue to personify for them, interpretation on the objective level is also important. Objective-level interpretations—taking the appearance of the dead in dreams as actually referring to the ongoing life of the dead—re-establish the link with the ancestral dimension of the soul and place the dreamer in the midst of the human meanings which are native to his soul. It is not a question of promoting occult thinking or superstitious beliefs. The dead have become the culture of the bereaved and as such have an objective imaginal form. They are not the wish-fulfillments of the inconsolably bereft. Nor are they hyper-cathected libidinal trends, introjects which make the letting-go less severe, or personal complexes. They are themselves, perhaps even more so now than we ever knew them to be. If we fail to recognize and give place to their objective reality they will become attenuated by our subjectivity. The exclusive use of subjective-level interpretations, or worse, reductive interpretations based on the Oedipus-complex, can corrupt the soul-making process and cause it to collapse into identification. Deadened in our own lives by our failure to restore the dead to life, we become, as it were, the living dead. The capacity to imagine death, a capacity that is given to us by the dead through our mourning of them, is what allows us to imagine life. Indeed, if we cannot find their souls after death we will lose our own even as we live. To flee from death is to flee from life as well.

From a psychological point of view, the objective-level interpretation of bereavement dreams works the psyche in a similar manner as does subjective-level interpretation in dreamers who are *not* bereaved. Interpreting the images of the dreamer's living companions on the subjective level voids the images of their outer lives, freeing their psychic or angelic value, their meaning for our death [11, pp. 97-104]. Rather than locking the dream-figures into the incarnational world by linking them to the outer persons with whom we live, move, and have our being, subjective-level interpretation treats them as metaphors or shades. Severed from their outer referents, the images are made available for soul-making in manner not unlike the images of those who have actually died. Indeed, to imagine the image of an outer being as an inner, subjective factor is to mourn it, or, rather, to mourn by means of it. As Hillman has pointed out, without a religious or imaginal culture rich enough to carry our imaginations, we force our friends and loved ones to be its bearers.[5] Then, when they let us down, as they inevitably must, we stamp and storm, not realizing that what has actually let us down is the bankruptcy of our culture. But just as the ancestors can

[5] "Relationships . . . are overloaded with archetypal demands. What people expect of mothers and fathers, teachers, friends and lovers is far beyond the ability of personal human beings; people ask that archetypal qualities be present in each other which . . . are present in only Gods and Goddesses" [3, p. 192].

come for a lost loved one, *epistrophe*[6]—reversion through likeness—can link the dream-figures which have been construed as subjective traits by subjective-level interpretation to the archetypes. Once this is accomplished, once we have an awareness of the mythic forebears of our dream-figures, we need no longer force our living companions to play archetypal roles.

Jung, who himself interpreted the dreams of the bereaved on the objective level, especially if he could not establish any compensatory reason for the images of the dead to be read subjectively, advised caution in this practice. The bereaved, Jung felt, can occasionally become fascinated with the dead and draw too close to their domain. A pastor who had lost a brother in a car accident in Africa and had held conversations in his dreams with his late brother wrote to Jung about his experiences. Jung recognized the experiences to be authentic encounters with the deceased, and hence, experiences that should not be "psychologized." In his rather lengthy reply, Jung sketched out his thoughts on the relative spacelessness and timelessness of the unconscious, as well as some of the eastern notions about postmortem psychic states, and then advised the pastor to respect the boundary that divides the living from the dead [9, p. 258]:

> With regard to contact with your brother, I would add that this is likely only to be possible as long as the feeling of the presence of the dead continues. But it should not be experimented with because of the danger of a disintegration of consciousness. To be on the safe side, one must be content with spontaneous experiences. Experimenting with this contact regularly leads either to the so-called communications becoming more and more stupid or to a dangerous dissociation of consciousness.

Making a place for the dead and re-establishing the ancestral dimension of the soul does not mean we must attempt to follow them into the beyond. The *abaissment du niveau mental* (Janet) required to perpetuate this kind of direct encounter may be too damaging for consciousness. While it is important to widen consciousness away from

[6] "Reversion through likeness, *resemblance*, is a primary principle for the archetypal approach to all psychic events. Reversion is . . . a method which connects an event to its image, a psychic process to its myth, a suffering of the soul to the imaginal mystery expressed therein. Epistrophe, or the return through likeness, offers to psychological understanding a main avenue for recovering order from the confusion of psychic phenomena . . ." [11, p. 4].

personal subjectivism by imagining the dead, it is also important not to allow consciousness to be dissolved in the beyond through a mediumistic imitation of the dead. Indeed, as Jung suggests in his "mythology of death," consciousness, or more particularly the ability to form clear cognitions, is the great advantage the living have over the dead, and for that very reason it is the greatest tool through which to honor their ends. The task of the living is to value the dead and to love and be loved by them into culture. Though the grief of bereavement may cause us to value our lives less, our lives are enormously important—especially to the dead. Only by living our own lives, here on this side of dying, can we offer the sacrifices which our lost loved ones require.

MOURNING AS THERAPY

As Jung states [12, p. 24]:

> Heaven has become for us the cosmic space of the physicists, and the divine empyrean a fair memory of things that once were. But "the heart glows," and a secret unrest gnaws at the roots of our being. In the words of the *Voluspa* we may ask: "What murmurs Wotan over Mirmir's head? Already the spring boils. . . .

It is perhaps indicative of the materialism of modern society that mourning has been conceptualized as the process by which we let go of "lost objects." Having lost our sense of the soul, we tend to view death as extinction, and regard mourning accordingly. While other ages were supported by their beliefs about the afterlife, today, more and more, we are bereft of these ideas. Trivialized by our fear of death, and committed to values which increase our sense of worthlessness, we attempt to find the significance of our lives in the transitory fashions of the day. But fifteen minutes of fame, which Andy Warhol assures us will be ours, is chilly comfort.

Perhaps the loss of soul to which modern man has fallen prey is a function of the rapidity of change. In this century, so much has come into being and passed away that there has not been sufficient time to mourn it. While the ancient Egyptians made objects for eternity and took them with them into their tombs, most of the objects we make are obsolete before we have even had an opportunity to become attached to them. Things today are made to be thrown away. Perhaps we begin to think of people this way too.

Modern man, hollow man, no longer inhabits the culture which his forebears made with their ancestors. The marvelous shell of outer death which was created when the first mourner attempted to do something on behalf of the dead and which has been refined ever since has been smashed in this century by modern man's insatiable thirst for more and ever more stimulation. "Heap[s] of broken images" lie strewn across the "wasteland." Though we pick up the pieces and write dissertations about them, we have neglected to piece together the shell and reinhabit it. We preserve those bits and pieces of the past in museums and libraries instead of allowing them to preserve and protect us. We look at the dead in glass-cabinet displays rather than deriving our sentience from them and seeing by means of them. We have made a science out of the past, when in reality it is an art.

Jung, in the passage quoted above, writes of the decline of religious culture that has accompanied the ascent of science. While all other ages before our own recognized gods in some form, in our age the gods have died from neglect and remain unmourned. We dared, once, to look directly into the face of God without benefit of a protective shield, and were so overwhelmed by what we saw that we were compelled to declare God dead rather than perish ourselves. And now, as we pretend that he is not there, as we ignore him, he lapses further and further into seeming extinction. But, of course, gods do not die, they merely change the place of their habitation. In Jung's view, the "unparalleled impoverishment of symbolism" which characterizes the present age is the malaise responsible for our "rediscover[y] [of] the gods as psychic factors, that is, as archetypes of the unconscious" [12, p. 23]. What once had been experienced as spirit, and given "a local habitation and a name" through imaginal culture, now stirs uneasily in the depths of our inflated self-importance. While Jung would concur with Eliot's diagnosis of hollowness, he also saw the possibility for a cure. Emptiness in one area implies fullness in another. Though the stars have fallen from the heavens, the waters below, the waters of the unconscious, are teeming with life. Spiritual renewal is still possible if we will but mine our impoverishment for its latent richness. Bereft of God, all we are left with is the metaphor of his death. Perhaps this rich metaphor will serve as the protective veil we must use to get reacquainted with him, for it is in mourning for his death that we will find his essence.

Ironically, despite thousands of years of civilization and millions of years of evolution we are now as alone in the face of death as were the first human beings. Though we continue to study culture we no longer recognize it as the life of the dead. The adage of the rapidly vanishing tribal societies of the twentieth century—"The gods leave the island when the anthropologists arrive" (cited in [13, p. 235])—is true of our "advanced" societies as well. By playing anthropologist to ourselves, by studying our culture as science, rather than consecrating it as an offering to the dead, we have banished the dead from their realm. In our zeal for abstraction we have betrayed the essential metaphors of our culture by taking them metaphorically.

But fortunately death is literal enough to start us metaphorizing again. Despite the emptiness of our souls, the loss of a dear one can give us substance once more. Through the spontaneous elegies of the bereaved, and with the help of the dead, the imagination resurrects itself on the other side of dying. Gradually, the underworld returns, the heavens fill with angels, and the ancestors lend dimension to our lives. As great "Death makes his darkness beautiful" in the people that we mourn, the soul achieves the splendor of this culture once again.

If, as Eliot said, the end of all our exploring will be to arrive at the place where we began and know it for the first time, let us end this exploration with the pre-historic grief of the *first mourner* [14, p. 93]:

> . . . primordial man, full of awe and horror, realizing death as death, [experiencing] the devastating shock that brought the first awareness of himself, the shock that began to make him human—the awakening of the instinct of reflection, the beginning of psychic life, culture, and religious belief.

To this pre-sentient being we offer thanks for his discovery of the soul and his legacy of sentience. To this pre-cultural being we owe an enormous debt of gratitude, for, through his love of the dead, he made culture—and all that we enjoy today—possible. To him we dedicate this elegy. Blessed in his mourning, may he teach us hollow men to praise.

REFERENCES

1. R. M. Rilke, *Letters of Rainer Maria Rilke, 1910-1924*, J. B. Green and M. M. Herter (trans.), W. W. Norton, New York, 1949.

2. F. W. Kaslow, Children Who Sue Parent: A New Form of Family Homicide, in *Journal of Marital and Family Therapy, 16*:2, pp. 151-163, 1990.

3. J. Hillman, *Loose Ends: Primary Papers in Archetypal Psychology*, Spring Publications, Irving, 1978.

4. T. S. Eliot, *Collected Poems 1909-1962*, Farber & Farber, London, 1974.
5. C. G. Jung, *Memories, Dreams, Reflections*, A. Jaffe (ed.), R. and C. Winston (trans.), Random House, New York, 1961.
6. S. Freud, *Beyond the Pleasure Principle*, J. Strachey (trans.), W. W. Norton, New York, 1961.
7. G. Mogenson, *God Is a Trauma: Vicarious Religion and Soul Making*, Spring Publications, Dallas, 1989.
8. A. Jaffe, *Apparitions: An Archetypal Approach to Death Dreams and Ghosts*, Spring Publications, Dallas, 1978.
9. C. G. Jung, *Letters, Vol. 1: 1909-1950*, R. F. C. Hull (trans.), Princeton University Press, Princeton, 1973.
10. M-L. Von Franz, *On Dreams and Death*, E. X. Kennedy (trans.), Shambhala, Boston, 1987.
11. J. Hillman, *The Dream and the Underworld*, Harper & Row, New York, 1979.
12. C. G. Jung, *The Archetypes of the Collective Unconscious, Collected Works*, Vol. 9i, R. F. C. Hull (trans.), Princeton University Press, Princeton, 1968.
13. H. Kalweit, *Dreamtime and Inner Space: The World of the Shaman*, W. Wunsche (trans.), Shambhala, Boston, 1988.
14. R. Lopez-Pedraza, *Hermes and His Children*, Daimon Verlag, Einsiedeln, 1989.

Index